OWN IT!
Love What You Already Have

SHEFALI KARANI

Own It! Love What You Already Have
First published in 2018
Copyright © 2019 Shefali Karani

ISBN
Print: 978-0-6483544-4-4
Ebook: 978-0-6483544-5-1

All rights reserved. No part of this book may be reproduced, stored in a retrieval system, or transmitted by any means (electronic mechanical, photocopying, recording, or otherwise) without written permission from the author.

Because of the dynamic nature of the internet, any web addresses or links contained in this book may have changed since publication and may no longer be valid. The information in this book is based on the authors' experiences and opinions, the views expressed in this book are solely those of the author and do not necessarily reflect the views of the publisher, and the publisher hereby disclaims any responsibility for them.

The author of this book does not dispense any form of medical advice, legal, financial or technical advice either directly or indirectly. The intent of the author is only to offer information of general nature to help you in your quest for personal development and/or self-help, in the event you use any of the information in this book the author and the publisher assume no responsibility for your actions. If any form of expert assistance is required, the services of a competent professional should be sought.

Publishing information
Publishing, design and production facilitated
by Passionpreneur Publishing
www.PassionpreneurPublishing.com

Testimonials

"I met Shefali Karani in 2017 at the Columbia Business School Women in Leadership program. I was impressed with her fluent style of leadership. She is a conscious leader with an enterprising spirit, and evolving the role of women in the corporate space. We share many similar values and philosophies of life. I have no hesitation recommending Shefali's inspiring story. She is an emerging leader—modern and wise."

- **Dr. Sophia N. Johnson**
Political Economist, Columbia University

***

"The journey towards becoming a CEO is never easy and smooth. Shefali's book provides an exciting account of a young woman's drive to become an executive at the age of 21 and her ascent to the respected posts of board director for three companies and business director for two companies in Mumbai, India. We learn a lot about her challenges, but primarily admire her leadership and determination to succeed."

- **George Tsetsekos**
*Francis Professor of Finance and
Dean Emeritus, Drexel University*

***

"Shefali is a keen observer and fast learner. She is meticulous, patient, and open-hearted, enabling a seamless transformation from stress to Zen. Wishing her the best in all of her endeavors."

- **Geeta Ramakrishnan**
*The Change Coach and author of
The Game of Change*

***

"I have been training Shefali since she was in college, and have observed one thing about her which is her strength and dedication. She is a fast learner; she picks up what's taught to her with complete attention. This is what made her stand out amongst others. Whichever field she stepped in, she didn't step back, although many emotional events do occur in every individual's life (a close relative expiring, getting married, etc.). She was like a spider climbing up after every fall with more speed. I wish her the best of luck and want her to keep away from worrying about the lightbulbs."

- Tehsin Ratna
Founder of the TV Show Get Fit &
TR Fitness, Mumbai, India

***

"In 2017, I had the opportunity to meet Shefali who came to me with a desire to explore opportunities to develop as a professional leader in her business community and as a female role model. She attended our programs at Columbia Business School Executive Education and achieved her Certificate in Business Excellence in just under a year. With the determination and openness to collaborate with others, she forged a new path for herself while supporting many of the global participants she met in our world-class professional development programs at Columbia. I believe she will continue to make an impact and always strive for more while generously supporting others."

- Jennifer Goez
Director of Learning Solutions,
Columbia Business School, Columbia University

***

Dedications

I dedicate this book to my husband, Bhavesh; to my parents; and to my little sister, Nikita. I also dedicate this book to my grandparents, Mom and Nana; and my uncle, Vyomesh Mama. Lots of love to my canine pals, Cookie and Charlie Brown. Thanks for all your support! Love you guys.

Acknowledgements

I want to acknowledge my husband, Bhavesh, for supporting me in writing this book. You've always been there for me, no matter what. You're my rock.

I would also like to thank my sister, Nikita, for giving her feedback on my book. Without you, this book would not have been possible. You reminded me that I had so much more to write about.

I would like to thank my parents for supporting me through the tough times in my life. It's because you both believed in me that I have become the strong leader that I am today. I would not be where I am now without your love and support.

I want to thank my grandmother whom I lovingly call "Mom." Mom, you've been an amazing role model for me. I am so inspired by you and your field of work. You helped me become the woman that I am today.

I would also like to thank Geeta Ramakrishnan, my life coach and friend, whom I fondly call "Aunty." Aunty, thank you for giving me some insights for this book and for helping me become more confident as a businesswoman.

A big "thank you" to Moustafa Hamwi of Passionpreneur Publishing. Thank you for believing in me and in this book. Your feedback and guidance have been invaluable throughout.

Contents

	Introduction	11
1	The Beginning	13
2	Change Is Good	31
3	Embrace Your Goals	43
4	Know When to Fight	53
5	Perfection in Imperfection	65
6	Keep Going	77
7	Using Anger as a Tool	91
8	Helping Others	103
9	Accepting Things as They Are	113
10	Go with the Flow	125
	Afterword	139
	About the Author	141

Introduction

Any of you who were born into a business family know that a family-owned business works quite differently from others. Since this was my situation, I had to constantly prove to others that I could be a capable leader once the reigns of the business were handed over to me.

Ever since I was a kid, I've been working tirelessly to be the best that I can be, whether it was at school, at college, or even at home. Some people always believed I was entitled; that I got whatever I wanted when I asked for it, but that's not true.

It may look like I had my life handed to me on a silver platter, but life is not easy in a family business. Becoming an executive at the age of twenty-one pushed me unexpectedly into the corporate family business world. Overwhelmed by the responsibilities I was given at the time, I learned to become a more confident and dynamic businesswoman.

I dealt with a lot of pressure to be the best person I could be, whether this involved being the best manager or the best student. I worked many late nights at school to keep up with everything and pushed myself to join the one-year MBA program at my school a few years later. I graduated with my Bachelor's degree *cum laude* and received numerous other accolades at the time. There were a lot of expectations that I needed to fulfil and even bigger shoes that I needed to fill.

At work, I dealt with certain challenges, learned a lot of lessons, and changed as a person. Working at a family business comes with its own set of challenges, and to navigate through that takes a lot of hard work. I learned a few lessons that will resonate with others working in a family business environment.

It may look like my life was all laid out for me, but it really wasn't. With the lessons I learned and the challenges I faced, I learned that I had to decide for myself. You can decide who you want to be, and with these lessons and my experience behind them, you too can learn what it takes to own it.

1

The Beginning

Twenty-one: the age I became an executive in my family's business. Twenty-one: the age when I also started to handle some of our companies' operations, including some work for our publicly-listed companies. To a twenty-one-year-old, that's a lot of responsibility! With only my Bachelor's degree in hand and help from my parents, I proceeded to work my way through the companies.

At twenty-four, I started my MBA; I finished it a year later. At twenty-eight, I officially became a board director, not just for one company, but for two of them. A year later, I got my CIBE from Columbia Business School, making me an Ivy League graduate. How did I do all of this before I turned thirty? By embracing change. That's how I became a businesswoman, muse, and philanthropist.

Nineteen. That's the number of times I changed houses. This definitely goes beyond the norm for anyone I know. People's responses to this statistic have ranged from laughter to pure amazement. I don't think anyone actually understood why I chose to do this. The fact that I not only changed houses so many times, but also moved to three different countries still astounds everyone to this day. A family business is what started it all.

It all started long ago when I was about five or six years old. My parents, my little sister, and I were packing our boxes to move to India from the United States. When we got there, half our luggage was lost, including some of my favorite toys. I was devastated. I had no friends, I was in a new country, I didn't really speak the language, and I had no toys.

A few years and a few schools later, I made some friends and learned a lot about the city of Mumbai. It was then that I also learned about our family business and the reason why we moved so much.

This was just the start of my beautiful journey of change. A few years later, we decided to move to Dubai in the U.A.E., since my family business was being divided. This is quite normal in big family businesses, but, as a kid, I didn't understand a thing. As I was preparing myself yet again to change houses, sadness crept in. My father told my sister and me not to worry; we would make new friends again in Dubai. But I tossed and turned in bed that night, wondering, "Why? Why me? Why can't I just live life like a normal kid?" This question bothered me every time we moved, until the day I learned to accept it.

Later, I started to accept the inconvenience of moving; I learned to tolerate it. Those who remain my friends until today know how much we moved without advance notice. Every time my dad had an important thing to tell us, we knew it was time to move again.

No sooner did we get to Dubai than we moved back to Mumbai within a couple of years. Then we headed back to Dubai again for my last two years of high school. While applying to colleges, it was hard for me to explain the situation I was in. I was not American but not Indian either. I had stayed in Dubai for a few years, but it was all still new to me. I knew English but not Arabic. I knew French but not Spanish. I knew Hindi but not Marathi. I understood basic spoken Gujrati and basic spoken Sindhi, but could not speak, read, or write in either language. I was as confused as ever. I had no idea what I wanted to do. I had no idea of my true identity—the person I wanted to be—other than the fact that I was a Ramsinghani.

I was also one pretty angry teenager. I was upset about the way I was—pathetic and severely low in self-esteem—since I hardly had any friends at the time. I had almost no confidence in myself and even believed that I would amount to nothing better than the person I was then. I went from having no career goal in mind, hardly any college choices at hand, and a bitterness from being constantly bullied at school to a teenager who wanted to change for the better.

At the time, I was dealing with all sorts of bullying, including virtual bullying, bullying at school, and bullying from some of my so-called friends. Chat messengers had just been introduced when I moved to Dubai, and people started using them as a means to keep in touch. As I started to make friends, they added me to their messenger list and started talking to me online. A few bullies even went as far as calling me a "lowly bitch" and a "good-for-nothing motherfucker with nuts." Some classmates called me weird for not wanting to go out with them or not partying; they ostracized me online. Sometimes, even after I blocked that person, he or she would create a new account and start bothering me all over again.

There would often be anonymous messages from classmates I knew, and there was no way to figure out who was sending what with their fabricated chat names. It was a whirlwind of cyberbullying, and it didn't stop until I finally started to fight back.

"Cunt," said one classmate.

"Sure, I am," I told him. Blocked.

"You're a bitch," yet another messaged me.

"Thanks." Blocked.

As time went on, there was less and less random bullying online, but that didn't mean the students at high school were going to stop bullying me in person.

During my last few years of high school, an unfortunate incident happened; I burnt my face. I had gone to a beauty salon to get my usual facial waxing routine done, and I was supposed to go to the gym in the same building later on. I sat in the room, and as the beautician started heating up the wax, I felt a little uneasy. Something in my gut was telling me to run from there. Alarm bells were ringing in my head. As soon as she spread the hot wax onto my face, I felt like I was on fire. When she removed the wax strips, I felt something peel off.

I ignored my gut feeling and went on upstairs to the gym. When I started working out, I felt a burning sensation on my face.

"Something's not right," I told my trainer.

As we both went to the washroom to see what was bothering me, I noticed three big red patches of raw flesh on my face.

"MY FACE!!" I screamed.

"How did this happen?" my trainer asked me.

"I don't know. I was at the beauty salon before, and now I see this!"

"Let's go there," my trainer said, and she grabbed my hand.

We went to the salon, and showed them what had happened. As the manager came up to us, my mother also came there to see what all the commotion was about. Nothing could be done, and the beautician was let off with just a warning.

That night, my mother called my grandmother who was a doctor, and asked her what to do. She applied burn cream on my face and I fell asleep. I woke up with a burning fever, and went to the doctor.

"You have some first-degree burns and a slight second-degree burn on your face," the doctor told us. "It will go away after a month or so. Keep applying the cream and wear a hat and shades when you go to school. The cream has to be kept on the whole day."

Happy to know that I did not require any surgery, I went off to school the next day.

"Hi, why are you wearing a hat?" the principal asked me as I walked into the school. Hats were against the dress code.

"I burnt my face."

"How?" the principle asked me.

"Someone at the mall spilled coffee on me," I lied. I did not want anyone to know what had really happened; I was embarrassed.

When I walked into my first period class, one of my greatest enemies—a girl who always bullied me—came up to me. She saw me with slimy cream all over my face and my skin peeling.

"What happened?" she laughed.

As I proceeded to tell her my story, she turned away and laughed. "She's no longer beautiful!" she told her friends, laughing away.

I sighed and sat down. For the next couple of weeks, I had random people come up to me and ask me what had happened. Most of them simply wished me well, while a few laughed at the predicament I was in.

Eventually, the burn marks faded away and all was forgotten. I still have slightly discolored facial skin to this day, but I am lucky that it is hardly noticeable.

Burning my face taught me how to deal with all sorts of bullying. I learned how to put on a brave face and kept going to school, despite how uncomfortable I was. I learned how to still be myself and continue studying without any issues.

That year, I was on the Honor Roll. I knew I could accomplish anything I set my mind to as long as I believed that I could. It didn't matter whether I had a pretty face or not. Confidence comes from within.

I was in a karate class during my senior year of high school. I was the only girl in a class full of macho boys. One day, my teacher challenged us all to a friendly karate match, with headgear for protection from the karate punches and kicks.

"You two, start fighting," my teacher told me and this other guy. That guy happened to be one of my arch-enemies at the time.

"Sure," he smiled coyly and headed towards the center of the floor.

"Great," I thought to myself.

"Fight!" my teacher yelled.

As I started defending myself and trying to get in a few punches, the guy kept hitting my face, smirking at me angrily.

"Argh!" I shouted as he hit me squarely on the helmet.

"Okay, enough!" my teacher yelled. I walked away, sweat dripping down my face.

"Good match," the guy told me, laughing.

"Sure," I told him.

"I'm really sorry about hitting you in the face. You were a good fighter," he said.

Astonished, I wiped the sweat from my face with my sleeve and faced him. "No worries. It's just a friendly match," I said and walked away.

I was hoping that he would apologize or say something more to make things better between us, but that was just wishful thinking on my part. I knew one thing for certain though; he wasn't going to bother me anymore.

At that moment, how did I know he wouldn't bully me anymore? Well, even though he tried punching me in the face and directed all his anger towards me, I didn't back down. I didn't give in, I kept on fighting, and I didn't care if I fell down or got hurt. I knew I wouldn't anyway, since my teacher was standing right there.

My opponent and I were both purple belts in karate, and I knew we both had to follow the rules or face the consequence: getting expelled from school. As high school seniors, that wasn't an option for us because graduation was just a few weeks away. Everything changed once I started to believe in myself.

The day I had my interview for Drexel University was the day my life changed. At the time, I was an overweight, short kid with a ton of acne and zero confidence. I had no clue about what I wanted to do with my life. I was a nobody. I was nervous as ever and didn't know what to say to the interviewer. I was at a loss.

I had just flown in from Dubai to Mumbai for this university interview. My parents told me at the last minute that a university I had applied to wanted to interview me in Mumbai. The interviewer knew I had school that day, but we got permission to leave early and fly to Mumbai.

When I reached the hotel where the meeting was taking place, I paced the lobby with my parents. I was wearing a nice formal shirt and a pencil skirt.

"I'm so nervous," I told them.

"You'll be fine. Just be yourself," my mother told me.

My dad was there as well. "The first impression is the most important," he told me. With that thought in mind, I felt a little more at ease knowing that this was the first interview, and I could be whoever I wanted to be from now on.

The moment I walked into the meeting room, something in me stirred. I knew that this was it. I knew that I was much more than what others had told me I was. I knew I was much more than the person who I was at that moment. I wanted to be this amazing person that I knew I could be.

As I walked through the double doors, I made up my mind. "I'm going to be a better person. I am going to be a successful businesswoman. It's now or never!" I told myself over and over again. I was tired of feeling sorry for myself. "I don't want to continue this pity party," I told myself. "It's not making me feel any better and is actually making me feel a lot worse. It's high time I got out of this rut and moved forward."

"I really want to be the best that I can be and not this cowardly person who is afraid of talking to others," I told myself. "I'm simply afraid of my own potential. I want to show the world just how confident I really am. I know I have confidence in myself. All I need is a little push in the right direction."

I got out of my comfort zone and mentally prepared myself for the interview ahead. "Great, now I have no idea how I'm going to do this. I'll just see what happens and go with the flow of things. If I'm supposed to get into this university, I'll get in for sure, without much effort."

"Why should we let you come to our university?" the interviewer asked me.

"I'm a go-getter," I told her as I smiled confidently.

Not only did I impress the interviewer a great deal, but I also got my college admission on the spot.

A few years down the line, I became an executive business director at my family's companies. Since I got married, I now work from Dubai while going for major meetings to Mumbai. Of course, I do go back to the United States to reconnect with my friends and family there. But the real question is this: how did I, a nobody, do all this? All I had to do was embrace change. That force then became a catalyst that helped me balance my life.

Own It!

Some people think I just had this job handed over to me on a silver platter, but I had to work really hard to be where I am today. I had to show my worth as a future executive and earn my job. That required a ton of self-transformation and belief. I also needed a lot of positive thinking to move my life in the right direction.

Before I even started working for the companies, I had to do an independent study for my university class in order to learn more about what I was going to be dealing with. That month was pretty tiresome. As I attended the office in Mumbai during my school break, I made it my mission to find out as much information as possible about that company for my class. I found out how the company was conceived, how it grew and developed, and everything else that a manager in the making needs to know.

I would write my paper for the class and report back to my class mentor, and he would direct me on what information to find for my own benefit. I spoke to numerous people within the company and did a lot of research. After I finished my paper, I finally realized just how much I had learned about the company.

I then became fairly knowledgeable about the inner workings of this company. With knowledge came confidence. I understood how the company worked, so I also felt that I would be able to start off my basic job at the office after I graduated from college.

After I graduated, I started work right away. I was a bit quiet and unsure of myself, for good reason. I was a young woman in a predominately male workplace, and I was an Indian

American. I had a very different accent from everyone else, although my Hindi was good. I would feel embarrassed by the way I sounded. I hadn't really lived continuously in Mumbai; I had spent part of my life in Dubai and the U.S.

Silk shirts and trousers were what I wore, along with the occasional print dress, yet I was not very confident in the way I dressed. Since I didn't really know my place in the company, I dressed like an outsider—a person who was sitting on the sidelines waiting to be called to the front.

"You need to dress in a more businesslike manner," my dad would tell me. "You need to look presentable, neat, and clean. How about you try wearing a crisp white shirt and a pair of black trousers? You'll look a lot better."

And so, with a work-wardrobe overhaul, I started dressing like an executive in the making. With a classic watch, some good jewelry, my hair combed, and dressed in a dapper outfit, I was ready to conquer the business world. My confidence rose, and I transformed from a newly-graduated college kid to a business pro.

People started greeting me at meetings, and soon, my presence was acknowledged. When I walked into the office, people would smile at me. My dad is the same way. He can command the attention of a room by just walking into it, even if he's wearing shorts and a t-shirt in a restaurant. His posture exudes confidence. The way he walks is confident. The way he talks is confident. People know that he is important the moment he walks into a room. He is a true leader. By viewing him as a role model, I began to imagine how I could command such attention from others.

As I walked into the office day after day, I started walking straighter and a little more confidently than the day before. I would smile and greet everyone as I walked by. I was no longer afraid of making a mistake. Even when I did make a mistake, my dad was the first one to correct me, but only when everyone else was out of earshot. I soon started to shadow my dad as he had asked me to. It's a great way to learn how things get done from the upper management's perspective.

After shadowing my dad, I started going for some factory visits. I would go around the factories with my dad, quietly observing what was happening and how things worked. I was very intrigued by the way the factories ran. I also developed a keen interest in how things worked. As I started to ask more and more questions, I also gained a lot of insight and knowledge about the manufacturing world. Extra report copies were soon given to me, and I would look at the financials, new project developments, and our future vision. Attending board meetings, general meetings, and other company meetings as an observer, I learned a lot about the companies my family owned. I also learned how to act around other businesspeople, and how to portray myself as a young businesswoman.

Initially, I would talk to my dad about any issues that I came across at work, but soon, I overcame that. "I'm going to be an executive," I would tell myself, even though I was nowhere close to being so (or so I thought at the time). Graduating *cum laude* from a good American university did not guarantee that I was going to become a good businesswoman or that people would even listen to my opinion. I had to prove myself time and again by being silent and by only speaking up when it was really necessary. Having an opinion on everything doesn't really help because I seriously wanted to point out everything that was right and wrong in the companies at the time.

Experience molds you into a good businessperson. I watched people being interviewed, people being promoted, and people being fired in front of me. At the time, I was a part of the management team with another manager who handled these sensitive issues, and I had to learn how to do that too. Reading reports and giving my feedback to my dad didn't always help, but once I got the go-ahead to do things on my own and handle a few projects, I gained confidence in myself, and so did everyone else at the company.

After I got promoted to executive, I was handling meetings and even certain projects on my own. My team would still correct me if I was wrong; this was helpful as it avoided future problems with the projects and helped me to gain their trust. As my team and colleagues reported back to me, we all started talking to each other even more than before. Soon, people would send me reports on their own and call me up on their own rather than waiting for me to ask them to do things. With my entrepreneurial skills from university and their experience from work, we were unstoppable. Our company's performance went through the roof that year, and we were all proud of our great teamwork together.

After two years of work experience, I decided to do my MBA. I needed some more credibility and knowledge if I wanted to become a business director in the future. Off I went to Philadelphia again. The one-year MBA program was tiresome indeed. I started in September that year and finished the next September. Our class hardly got any holidays besides a few basic ones; we had classes in the summer as well and before school even started.

B-school was tough. Applying to MBA programs at the age of twenty-four was tough. No one wanted a twenty-four-year-old with just two-odd years of work experience because I was too young. But, Drexel University saw my potential. After getting two wonderful recommendations from my past college mentors, and with my previous achievements in hand, (earning a Bachelor's degree, *cum laude*, with two majors and one minor is no easy feat) I managed to get an interview for the one-year MBA program.

In my apartment in Dubai, I prepared myself for my video interview with the MBA representative.

"You had some amazing recommendations!" the representative told me. "Being a Drexel alumna and a brilliant student, it's safe to say that you're in!"

I was jumping up and down for joy. I had applied to three B-Schools, two of which had already rejected me. I had almost lost all hope, but my college mentors had told me that I had a chance of getting into my old school since I had been such a star scholar there. They were right! Even though I applied last minute with no hope left, the confidence that they instilled in me shone through. That's how I got into the one-year program.

My MBA started. Classes were tough, and I was one of the

youngest students there. What started as a class of twenty-one students ended up as a class of just eighteen within the next few months. We only had a few classes in common with the normal two-year MBA class. Our cohort of eighteen grew strong. We went on a memorable international business trip to Vienna and Prague. We got through study sessions together, we worked on projects, we spent late nights studying, and we had countless coffee dates. We were a team.

The September we graduated, we were all emotional about it. I made so many good friends that are still with me today. Although I didn't get to attend my actual graduation ceremony that year as it was in June and I was with my family at the time (it was one of the few weeks that I had free), I felt connected to everyone in my class. The same feeling applies to work as well. When you feel connected to your team, communication just flows and good things start to happen at work.

After I became a business director for two of our companies, I knew that my MBA and work experience were not enough. I needed to learn more. It was then that I decided to apply for a class at Columbia Business School. Getting into the CIBE program for executives was unexpected. With my work experience, company position, and MBA knowledge, I managed to get into this prestigious Ivy League program. I also got into the Women in Leadership program since I was a young female executive.

The day I graduated from Columbia Business School was amazing. My program manager took some time off to come personally to my class and hand me my certification. "I'm so proud of this young, confident woman and what she represents," she told the class in a moving speech. My classmates applauded as I received my CIBE. I was finally an Ivy League graduate.

"Smile!" my mother said as I stood by the famous statue on campus. I was so happy that I did it! It took a lot of studying, hard work, time, and dedication, but I was able to complete all my classes in a year while working part-time.

"I got my CIBE from Columbia Business School," I told some of the board directors.

"Congratulations!" one of them said.

After that day, whenever I attended a board meeting, I felt more confident. I got my CIBE for myself, and along with that, others automatically appreciated my newfound confidence and newly-acquired knowledge. I felt that I was taken more seriously by others after this program. After all, how many executives have two degrees and one certification at the age of twenty-nine? Soon after my thirtieth birthday, I became a board director for one of our publicly-listed companies and I couldn't have been happier.

Change is all you need. It's a force of goodness. It's the catalyst that pushes us forward, makes us better people, and helps us balance our lives. It's this type of change that helps us accept the difficulties that come our way. Becoming an executive at a young age was no easy feat. No one was really willing to support me, besides my family. Choosing to work with my family was the hardest decision I ever made, but it was certainly the best.

2

Change Is Good

Why would change ever be good for us? Well, for starters, it helps you become a better person, and it helps you move forward in life. For a person who has changed houses nineteen times and lived in three different countries, change is an everyday occurrence.

Mumbai. A city with a million things happening at once. I had just finished my Bachelor's at Drexel and had come home to join the family business.

"You have to shadow me if you want to learn. It's the only way you'll learn." My father was very clear about this. I would not become a manager or take on any work responsibilities until I shadowed him for a year.

Disheartened, I became a silent observer. "Why can't this happen sooner?" I thought to myself.

But I was glad that I did shadow my father because, a few months later, I became an unofficial executive at work. Although it took time for others to accept the fact that I was young and didn't have a lot of work experience, I was able to appreciate it; I used it for getting things done. I used that criticism to better myself as an executive and to progress in my career. No sooner did I learn this than another problem came along.

"Why is she here? She's a woman. She should be at home," said an old man at our annual company meeting. As I stood there in shock, my father said nothing to him.

"Why in the world would you say nothing to him?" I asked my father. I was obviously upset.

"Well, it's okay. It's just his opinion," he said.

Turns out there were many more like this old man who were not appreciative of my being involved in my family's business. I then decided to change my attitude towards the people who were not so happy about my work presence. If anyone said something hurtful, I learned to just listen and walk away diplomatically. This wasn't always an easy thing to do, but I knew in my heart that I had to become tough or no one would ever take me seriously. No sooner did I master this technique than another issue arose: being a woman in the business world.

"You have two girls? You don't have any sons? What about the business? Who will look after it?" one woman asked my mother.

"Sons and daughters are equal to me," my mother replied calmly.

When I heard this, I was not surprised. My parents always

treated my sister and me as equals, and I always had their support. It's with their support that I was able to deal with issues of gender inequality at work with ease. As I continued to tackle these issues on a daily basis, I learned how to change and balance my life. But nothing would prepare me for what I was about to face next.

What was meant to be another meeting turned out to be a cruel revelation of how others viewed me. A businessman started discussing some new changes to the board requirements.

"Oh, I see you have a woman here already. I guess she's just here to fulfill the board quota, isn't she?"

Fuming inside and ready to yell back, I nevertheless remained silent.

"She's working with us, and she's managing one of our companies," said my father. The businessman fell silent.

At that moment, everyone in the meeting understood why I was there. I was there as a young businesswoman, not as a figurehead who would fulfill some new business rule. I knew this was bound to happen yet again, but since I had learned to accept change, I was better prepared to deal with such ignorant people.

Recently, we had another meeting. A spokesperson had come to talk to us about his company. While handing out brochures, he casually skipped me, and went on talking about his work. The meeting ended, and he handed everyone else his business card but still managed to ignore my presence.

I then spoke to my father briefly. The spokesperson noticed

we were talking.

"Hello, nice to meet you," he said.

"Okay, same here," I said.

This spokesperson changed his perspective in a matter of seconds because he realized his mistake. Had I not been willing to accept this change, I would have probably remained upset for no reason for the rest of the day. I would have also lost out on some good networking prospects. Change is good. It helps us move forward and balance our lives better.

High school: the worst years of my life. I was not self-confident at all. I was not the smartest person in the room either. As I struggled to gain a sense of identity, I came across a wonderful notion.

"Let's face everything head on," I told myself every single day.

Boy, was I wrong about this. I ending up sitting alone in a corner during my lunch break with a book in my hand. My mother used to feel sorry for me and came to visit me at times.

This pretty much summed up my last two years of high school. I was alone all the time. During this time of loneliness, I learned to appreciate being on my own and having no friends. This was when I truly understood who I was as a person and who I could be.

Own It!

While I read my books, I gradually began to realize that I liked being alone. Being alone was not a bad thing. In fact, it gave me the power to handle every situation that came my way. No friends? No problem. I used that time to get closer to my family and gain knowledge about the world out there.

It was with this change that I grew as a person and became who I am today. It was with this loneliness that I allowed change to come into my life. It was with this loneliness that I also gained power over my negativity. It was with this loneliness that I accepted the fact that it is lonely at the top as an executive.

Change is good even if it appears to be bad at first. Had I not faced such dire situations at the time, I would not be such a strong leader. I would not be able to lead myself or lead others on the right path. My life would have been chaotic and unbalanced beyond belief. I probably would have reverted back to my overweight, unconfident self if I still believed that change was bad. Change was a positive force in my life that propelled me to new heights—from a shy kid to a successful businesswoman.

In high school, I was an overweight kid with acne all over my face. I was shy and had no confidence while talking to others. I was constantly bullied since I didn't fit in and had only a handful of friends. At home, I would eat to my heart's content. Soon, I had to start exercising and go to a dietician.

"You know, you're close to being overweight," the dietician told me. "You have to do something about this or you're going to have a problem."

As I tried following the advice she gave me, I grew increasingly frustrated. I ate even more junk food and desserts and ended up being even heavier than before.

When I went to Mumbai for a holiday, a friend of mine started working out with a trainer. She recommended him to me, and soon, I started working out with the two of them. When school started, I went back to Dubai and got another personal trainer over there so that I could continue working out. I gave up my horrible junk food habit and started to eat more nutritious food, along with the occasional dessert or chocolate bar.

My first high school prom day came. As I walked to the dance floor, all eyes were on me.

"You look beautiful," one of my classmates said to me.

I felt like Cinderella. I had transformed from a nerd into a prom princess. I felt beautiful inside and out. That gave me the confidence to become even better than I was before, and I became an avid gym goer.

To this day, I make it a point to workout with personal trainers in Dubai and Mumbai, or on my own in the U.S. Being healthy is beautiful. It creates self-confidence and inner strength.

College was the time that I found my true self. I had confidence, I was at my optimal weight, and I dressed to impress. I became a part of a few academic clubs and the

Honors Program; I also took up a dual major as well as a minor. It was the time that I was the busiest.

Since I was graduating, my choir teacher allowed me to be a soloist for the U.S. national anthem, along with two other singers, on graduation day. That day, the Dean, who also happened to be the mentor for one of my academic clubs and an independent study that I had done, asked me to be on stage during graduation. He also asked me to be one of the first students on stage since I had achieved so many academic feats.

The next day, I went on stage to sing. My family sat in the front row and cheered me on. As I sang, the spotlight shone on me and the two other singers. At that moment, I sang my very best, and people applauded as I finished singing.

Beaming with happiness, I went off stage. A few minutes later, I was called on stage. With two medals, a few honor cords, and some other drapes on my shoulders, the president of the university handed me my graduation roll. People were clapping, and my friends and family were standing up and chanting my name. It was amazing; I couldn't believe that I had graduated as one of the top students in my class—*cum laude*, with honors and distinction. I had even gone for President Obama's inauguration during my junior year with a select few Honor Program students. How many students get to do that!

After graduation, my friend came up to me. "Wow, I didn't know you could sing! Congratulations on your amazing accomplishments." Many others congratulated me after this.

From that day on, I knew I had accomplished what I wanted to do. I became a star scholar in college. When I came back to the same university to do my MBA a few years later, professors came up to me. I was shocked that they even remembered me. They even went and told my sister who attended the same university that they knew me, long after I had graduated. I knew then that I had done something right; I had accomplished what I never thought I could, all because I believed in myself.

On the eve of my second engagement anniversary, a very random accident happened to me; I got a fork stuck in my hand. I was in Mumbai, having my lovely Sunday lunch which my cook had made for me, and my dad was sitting there as well. I picked up my napkin and felt a pinch on my left wrist.

"Shefali, you might want to look at your hand," my dad said worriedly. As I turned to look at my wrist, I saw that a fork was dangling from it.

"FUCK!" I said as I yanked the fork out.

"Sit down," my dad said as he rushed to get a first-aid kit and some medicine.

"I don't feel so good," I said. My vision started to swirl around me, and I felt my body breaking into a cold sweat.

"Have this," my dad said, handing me a glass of water and a painkiller.

The feeling of darkness soon passed, and as I sat there in

a weakened state, with a deep fork mark on my hand, my grandmother—the doctor—spoke to me on the phone. I was told that it was not a deep wound, and I was not required to go to the hospital then.

That day, my husband was at the hotel preparing for our flight back to Dubai. "Are you okay?" He rushed to my side as soon as he saw me.

"Yes," I told him weakly. I showed him the wound which was covered with a big bandage. When I reached the airport, I got a video call from my grandmother once more to show her the wound. As I was given the go-ahead to board my flight, I noticed my wrist had swollen substantially. On the flight, my wrist started to pain and throb. When we landed, my husband took me to the hospital.

I entered the emergency room, quite afraid of what would happen.

"Yes, what seems to be the problem here?" the receptionist asked.

"I had a little freak accident," I told him.

The nurse came up to me. "What happened?"

"I had a fork stuck in my hand," I said.

"Oh, a fork stuck in your hand!" she laughed.

"How is that funny?" I thought to myself.

When we spoke to the doctor, some serious questions were asked. "Are you sure nothing happened and that this was an accident?" the doctor asked my husband and me.

"Yes," I told her for the tenth time.

"Are you sure this happened by mistake?" she asked me.

"Yes," I told her firmly.

I later found out that these were just routine questions that were asked to make sure that my husband hadn't hurt me or that I had not tried to intentionally hurt myself. But these questions really bothered me until the day I got better.

The next day, I went to a doctor I knew. He was sensible and knew I was not the type to do such things. Neither was my husband the type to lay a finger on me. He told me that I was alright and that this was just a puncture wound. My nerves were intact since I was able to move my left hand.

He told me to take some painkillers and to do some physiotherapy exercises on my own until I got better. An MRI was not required since I was able to move. Yet, I was not able to drive for a few months, I could not lift anything heavy for a whole year, and I could not even move my left hand without a throbbing sensation in my wrist.

One of my grandaunts, who was also a doctor, met me in Mumbai when I went there for work a few months later.

"Let me see your hand," she said. As I showed her my wrist, she gasped. "You know, you're very lucky. The fork just missed your veins."

When I went home that day, I realized that I was fortunate to be alright after such a random accident. The scars are still on my left wrist today, but with time, the pain and marks have slowly faded away. The scars serve as a reminder that anything can happen in life. Had I not been willing to act and change the way that I was feeling the moment that the fork got lodged into my wrist, the outcome would have probably been worse.

If I were to go back and look at how I used to be, I would see that the old me could never have handled any of these problems. I would've probably run away from it all and blamed everyone for everything. I wouldn't be as proactive as I am now, and would definitely not be willing to face the challenges that I face today as a young executive.

Change is what made me who I am, and it's with this change that I learned to balance my life and created the life that I want now. It's with this change that I progressed so quickly in my career, and it's with this change that I am now willing to take risks. It's due to this change that I am only going forward, not backwards in my life. Change is powerful.

3

Embrace Your Goals

Twelve years old and locked in the restroom. A bunch of girls were bullying me and wouldn't let me out. I struggled to open the door but to no avail. As I watched the girls circle around me while I was still hiding in the bathroom stall, I wondered again, "Why me?" I had just changed schools, and now I had to deal with this.

The leader of the pack told me, "We're doing this because you deserve it."

I flung the stall door open and rushed past them as the school bell signaled the end of our lunch break. I made my way back to class, heart racing and thoughts running through my mind.

"Why did they do that to me?" I asked myself.

There was only one answer: I was different.

Being the oddball of the class was easy. Trying to fit in was hard. As the days went by with this scenario behind me, I began to question myself. What did I do to make those girls so mad? Was it really because I was different or because I was someone they were not? It turned out to be the latter. I was the person that they secretly wanted to be.

I came to terms with this bullying which continued for many more years at the different schools I attended. I realized that it was not a bad thing to do whatever I wanted, to just be myself. It was actually a splendid thing to be different.

When I was in high school, a couple of class incidents happened. In tenth grade in Mumbai, I had written a beautiful paper for my French class. That day, I was excited to get my grade for the paper.

As I entered the class, my teacher approached me. "You wrote this paper, right?" she asked me.

"Yes, I did," I said, smiling.

"Sure you did! Your tutor must have written it!" she yelled at me.

"But…" The bell rang, signaling the start of class, and my classmates arrived. I went to my seat and sat there, upset.

"Class, Shefali here has written a paper that is too good to be true. Please stand, Shefali."

I stood up, trembling. I had a tutor, but she was not the one who wrote the paper.

"Sit down, please. Everyone, start writing. We'll see how well you write now, Shefali."

I couldn't think, and as the teacher rambled on about the paper while we were all supposed to be writing it out, I could not, for the life of me, write anything properly.

A few days later, I asked the school counselor if I could switch to the lower level French class. Once I did that, I ran into my old teacher.

"You know that I wrote that paper, and you were wrong to call me out on that. I hope you know that," I told her.

She looked at me sternly, and then walked away.

I flourished in the new class I was in, and even the teacher knew I was right.

A few years later, during my last year of high school in Dubai, I had to write a presentation for my French class. I got up to start my presentation, and a couple of lines into the presentation, my teacher stopped me.

"Your presentation is atrocious. I cannot listen to it anymore. You get an F."

I stood there as my teacher criticized me in front of everyone. I tried to stop the tears from falling from my eyes, but I knew I couldn't. I sat there, silently crying for the rest of the class, my head spinning.

The next time I had a presentation, I chose a topic that I felt confident talking about, and I aced it. My teacher was surprised, but I knew he was only looking out for me. He wanted us all to speak French properly. I cannot thank him enough for what he did because it was he who seriously made me consider minoring in French once I got into college.

I got my minor in French as a part of my Bachelor's degree and am fluent in French. When I went to Paris recently for my wedding anniversary, I spoke in French, and no one even realized I was not Parisian.

The summer I graduated from high school was one to remember; I was happy and travelling with my family. I couldn't ask for more! I had then started to move into my dorm room in Philadelphia, and I intended to spend more time with my grandmother who also lived in the States.

When the car pulled up, adrenaline rushed in. The day was perfect. People swarmed around their cars, running around like ants. "This is it!" I told my mother and grandmother.

I walked swiftly towards the dorm, bag in tow. That feeling was amazing. I wish it could have lasted forever, but as life goes on, feelings always fade away. I really thought I had left the bullying behind, but college brought a new kind of bullying to light.

College days in Philadelphia were busy. Weekends were spent at home with my grandmother, and the school week was spent on campus. Halfway into the school year, I came across something that was quite alarming: college bullies.

"You're not Indian, you're American," one guy said to me.

"I'm from Mumbai," I replied.

This didn't really help my case. That particular group of people grew more and more averse to my presence, yet I couldn't avoid them. We were all in the same school and had common friends. It's really not easy to avoid such people.

One fine day, I couldn't take it anymore. I stormed out of my dorm room and decided to have a little talk with them. It was chilly outside, and as I walked to meet them in order to face my fears, I realized that it was no use talking to such idiots. I still managed to sit with all of them, smiling and pretending that everything was alright. It was tough but doable.

Although I chose to hang out with them and deal with their antics, I only did this so that I could overcome the crazy feeling of anger within me whenever they spoke to me around my friends.

"Hey, what's happening here?" I asked in Hindi when I met up with them before class. Did I startle them? Proving them wrong didn't help in any way, shape or form; it just gave me an ego high that day. It was from then on that I decided to work on my goals.

When I separated from that group of toxic friends, I decided to go all out. "I'm going to be the healthiest, prettiest, smartest person that I can be, and no one can stop me!" That was my chant to myself every day. To my surprise, I started going to the gym; I'm actually quite lazy and not a fan of any sort of exercise. The days went by.

On my way to the gym one day, I met one of the toxic friends from that group. He smiled to me and said, "Hey, what've you been up to?"

I walked past him quickly and said, "I've been busy with the Honors Program and choir. Byeee!"

As I ran across the courtyard to the gym, I couldn't help but smile. The look on that guy's face was priceless. He knew I had changed, and he knew I didn't give a damn about what any of them thought, Indian or not. I knew who I was. Goal one achieved.

Being healthy helped me balance my college life. It also helped me distinguish the good friends from the bad. I always make sure to keep in touch with my good friends and leave out the toxic ones.

The first year at college was tough. It was an eye-opening experience for all. Things got better the next year when I decided to change my sense of style a bit. Being a nerd didn't mean that I had to dress the part. I was constantly wearing clothes that made me feel fat and unconfident.

"I need a change," I thought to myself.

I was heading for my inauguration into the Honors Program. I had dressed up in a blue shirt and jeans with a pretty gold necklace. I felt good. When I entered the room, everyone was smiling at me. I felt like a million bucks. "So this is what it feels like to be confident," I thought to myself.

From that day on, I always dressed well during school. Looking your best doesn't mean wearing the most expensive or trendy outfit. It means dressing up in what you're confident wearing. Clothes make a person for sure, but only to a certain extent.

One college weekend, I decided to do some shopping at the

outlets near our home. I entered the boutique.

"Can I look at this shirt?" I asked the saleswoman.

No response.

"Uh, I need some help here," I said again.

The saleswoman looked straight past me. But when another customer walked into the store, she chirped, "Let me help you!"

I was furious. "She's really ignoring me?" I asked myself, "We'll see."

I wanted to tell her, "Lady, I have a personal shopper!" but that would have been really arrogant of me, even though it was true.

I walked out of the store, found my mother, and walked back into the store with her and a ton of bags in my hands. My mother knew what had happened and waited for the saleswoman to approach us.

"Let me help you guys!" the saleswoman said. The irony…

Later, as we were driving home, my mother had a heart to heart with me. "I know the saleswoman ignored you, but you need to know why. You can't ask me for help all the time."

"What went wrong?" I asked.

"You weren't dressed your best today. You're wearing a ratty old sweatshirt and jeans with your hair in a bun. I know you're not feeling your best either. Clothes make a huge difference. Always dress in what makes you look and feel good; then watch how the world reacts."

From then on, I vowed to always look my best no matter what day it was. Even when I'm at home, I make sure I'm wearing something I like—something which makes me feel like a superstar.

The third goal was the hardest: being the smartest I could be. I knew I was smart, but I didn't feel smart. I wasn't really embracing my goal even though I had gotten into the Honors Program. It was then that I decided to prove myself wrong. I worked long hours after my classes, and I joined a couple of academic clubs.

It was then that I started to realize why being different was such an asset. Being different helped me view the world in a whole new way. Not many people had the experiences that I did, and at that age, no one was willing to acknowledge their differences; they all wanted to fit in.

Months later, I stood at a podium. I was giving a speech on behalf of one of the academic organizations that I was a part of. All eyes were on me. "Wow, this is it," I told myself as I finished my speech. It came easily to me. But public speaking had not always been such a breeze.

In high school, I got stuck in a debate class. "You need to speak louder," my teacher would repeatedly tell me. I felt like a mouse. Then, one fine day, something very interesting happened. A classmate of mine decided to speak out against me, using some very sensitive information: how much money I had.

"Look at the car you have! You have so much money.

Hahaha," the boy said.

"Now then, please settle down," the teacher said, smiling.

"No, I'd like to talk about how much money she has," he said.

As the boy went on, the teacher grew helpless in his efforts to stop him.

Angry inside, I said, "So what!?! What does this have to do with anything in class?"

The boy shut up.

After class, I walked to my car. When my chauffeur opened the door, the same boy jumped in front of me, blocking my way. "This is your car! It's so special, so fancy! You spent so much on it. Ha-ha."

I walked to the other side of the car and got in.

A few months after graduation, a picture was posted on a social media site. It contained my car and its number plate with a caption for all to see, along with the name of a group that supported this endeavor. "We know who you are. We know you have money! Pay for my way back to Dubai!"

Needless to say, the post got removed soon after. I now know when to speak up, and I know how to talk loudly and firmly. With this incident, I gained the confidence that I needed to become a better speaker, and along with that, I felt and became smarter.

Goals are very important. Unlike New Year's resolutions which are broken, the goals that you make when there are upheavals in your life help you become the best that you can be. Without goals, you're like a bird in a cage; you have wings, but you can't fly anywhere. It's important to set new goals whenever you deal with a problem that refuses to move out of your way, just like that boy who refused to get out of my way when I was trying to get to my car.

Once you have certain goals in place, you can easily deal with change and have your life balanced out for you. It's not an easy thing to do, but when you put your mind to it, it's definitely possible. Circumstances in your life should not define you, but your goals should. Had I let such situations stop me from achieving my goals, I would've been stuck in the same place. I would've been quite miserable as well, despite the glorious self-pity I was indulging in at the time.

Goals create change. Change causes momentum. Momentum creates balance.

4

Know When to Fight

A mentor once told me that you have to act like an executive to feel like an executive, and that can only come through confidence. Confidence helped me decide when it was right to argue and when it was right to keep quiet. I learned to pick my fights wisely and also to let go of certain problems.

College days were a wondrous collage of good and bad. One event stood out in particular; I was standing in front of the class, giving a presentation during my final year. Confident and all dressed up in my best business clothes, there was no doubt that I was going to ace this. The room filled with applause after I was done.

After class, one of my classmates came up to me and said, "I can't realistically see how you're going to become a managing director, let alone a board director after just a few years. I don't think it's going to happen." He then started laughing at my presentation.

Appalled and speechless, I didn't know what to say. "Maybe

he's right, and I'm destined to fail. Who am I kidding with this career plan?" I said to myself.

I am glad to say that he was absolutely wrong about this, and I was happy that I didn't listen to him. Such people like to bring others down. Although this seems tough to digest, most successful people have to deal with it at the start. The resentment from envious people only grows as you become more successful.

Seven years old and trapped in a box. That was the first time I had to defend myself. My best friend at the time was pretending to be a magician and told me to hide in a box. The box was small and dark, and I waited patiently as she started her magic trick. A few minutes later, I was gasping for air.

"Get off the box!" I screamed at her.

She didn't listen; why would she? We were just seven-year-old kids. As innocent as her antic seemed, it was starting to take a toll on me. I pushed the box over and ran out. My friend sat there, dazed.

When I got home, I told my mother, "I never want to talk to her again! She put me in a box, and I could not breathe!" I was sobbing away.

An hour or so later, my friend and her mother came over to my house. "She has something to say to you," her mother told me.

"I'm really sorry…" my friend cried. "Can we still be best

friends?"

"Of course!" I said, and we became friends again. I didn't let anything silly like that box incident ever happen again. We're still good friends today and laugh about this box trick whenever it comes up.

Knowing when to fight is important, but knowing how to fight creates diplomacy.

The first couple of years at work were some of the toughest years I faced. People constantly wanted to fight with me, including some of my so-called friends. It was in the middle of the night during one of these years that a friend decided to lash out at me in the meanest way possible.

My phone was blinking on the table with a new text message while I was asleep. The light caught my eye and I awoke. "What did my friend message me at this time of the night?" I wondered. I opened the message to make sure she was okay. It turned out she was a bit drunk and had messaged me. As I replied, she continued sending me more and more angry messages.

Eventually, two hours later, she finally said what was on her mind. "You are all a bunch of nobodies. You guys aren't even famous and don't even come in the newspaper!"

With my sleepy eyes and even more tired body, my brain couldn't process this anymore. She was arguing with me because of who I was and what I was becoming. I couldn't believe my eyes. She was willing to put our friendship on the line because she was jealous of who I was! Angry and ready to defend myself, I furiously typed back, "My family doesn't need to be famous to be in a newspaper. I know who I am and so do you. Don't ever talk to me again."

Our friendship ended on bitter terms. Although I lost a dear friend, it was through her that I learned the most important lesson of all: knowing when to fight. I must admit that I was also a terrible friend for not seeing these tell-tale signs of jealousy in the first place. I should have spoken to her there and then about this before everything got out of hand. But at that time, I was a bit naïve about such things and didn't like confronting others. Sometimes when I see her around, we say hello or just smile at each other, but nothing more.

At first, it may seem really hard to figure out when to fight back and when not to. There's always going to be people out there, family and friends included, who will not support you, no matter what you do. Those are the types of people that are always going to fight with you, even if you do the right thing. This is when you need to decide who and what to fight for.

If someone cuts in front of me in a line, that's okay. At most, I'll politely tell them that there is a line, and that normally does the trick. If someone cuts in front of me while driving, that's fine too, and as long as we are both okay, it's not really worth letting my blood boil over. If someone speaks badly of me to others, that's also okay, but the moment it gets out of hand, I'll step in and do something about it.

An article was being published about me in a magazine. Swamped with work at the time, I hadn't even noticed when it came out. I opened my e-mail a couple of weeks later, excited to see it in print and online. Boy, was I disappointed. The page opened, and there, I saw a picture of some random woman with my name underneath it. I couldn't believe my eyes. Was this a joke? I know how serious magazines are about their articles, so it surprised me that they were so careless about this.

I spoke to the editor of the magazine. "Sorry, I didn't catch it," she told me apologetically.

Furious, I asked "Can't you do anything about this?"

"Nothing at all," she said. "The best I can do is reprint it with the right photo in the next issue. But I can't remove the picture from the online magazine. I'm really sorry."

Months passed by, and as I struggled to find the right person to get rid of the picture posted online, I started to lose all hope. I knew it was too late to get rid of the published version of the magazine but what about the online version? I didn't want my employees and friends seeing this huge mistake when they looked me up online. Neither did I want to press charges because of this silly mistake.

One evening, this issue reached new heights. The fact that the picture was online was always at the back of my mind. I also felt it was creating a negative situation for me. I decided to call the head of the organization. Although this seemed like a bold move, I knew it was the right thing to do.

As the lady argued with me on the phone, I made her see it from my point of view. Here I was, a young businesswoman and an Ivy League graduate, awaiting a TV interview. Since TV interviewers do a lot of research before your interview, it's important to have the correct information posted online. That article was one of my only good publicity pieces recently, and I felt that this silly mistake was ruining everything.

"How could you do this? Do you know how many people are going to see this?" I told her angrily. I had to say something in order to get them to take some action about that picture, and what I said was absolutely true. Of course, you can't go around putting random pictures of people on the internet like that. What message will that send to everyone else? I continued arguing with her and eventually reached a compromise. I understood that she was pressed for time, and it was an honest mistake, but I felt otherwise.

Because of what I thought was bad publicity (since it was the wrong picture) and also because I felt she was being slightly racist by posting a random picture of some other Indian American woman, I needed this change to happen. Once I finished talking to her, I calmly thanked her and all who were involved. A few days later, the picture was removed from their online site, and an apology was issued to their subscribers through e-mail. The right thing was done. Relief.

Bitterness aside, this situation taught me another lesson in knowing when to fight. You should always stand up for yourself when someone is trying to defame you, intentionally or not. Defamation can have some serious consequences for your career, even more so if you're scheduled for a TV interview soon, as was the case with me.

Weddings are joyous events that are cherished forever. My wedding was one to remember. As I got chosen to be a muse for designers and friends, an article was soon published about my wedding. I had multiple social media posts going up about my wedding, and I was asked whether designers, make-up artists and others who helped during the wedding could use my photographs.

Not everyone is going to appreciate the attention that another receives. As I got more attention about my grand wedding celebration and more and more offers to be a muse, some people grew envious of me.

"You guys spent so much on the wedding," one guy angrily told me. He had nothing to do with the wedding, but he still felt the need to say this.

A few months later, I met another person who said to me, "You only married your husband because of his fame and reputation. You married him for money."

Yet another person told me, "You have more money than your husband. Ha-ha!"

These are just some of the things that were said by a few others about my wedding and whatever was related to it. None of these statements are true as my husband and I married for love; we had met through a family friend. Yet, I found it a bit irritating to hear things like this from people every once in a while.

I knew I did the right thing by speaking up each time anyone ever said anything falsely related to my wedding, or the lies would've gotten even worse. But I have my limitations, and at some point, I draw the line. Nowadays, I don't really argue much when this is brought up because I find that it's a waste of time trying to prove a point to others. So, a bunch of people believe that my wedding was this, that, and whatnot but that doesn't mean that my wedding was actually like that or that my marriage was based on what anyone said.

It was based on a mutual decision—my husband's and my own—to get married. We treat each other as equals. My husband supports my work and understands that I often have to travel. That's what's truly important and not the opinion of others.

Recently, I was able to really see this lesson come into play. I was going to get some paperwork done at another organization. Everything went well until the moment I reached the lady at the counter. She looked confused when she saw my paperwork.

The supervisor came back, saying, "I'm sorry, this cannot be done."

"Why not?" I asked. "I have all the paperwork right here."

She walked away.

Confused and bewildered by her answer, I waited until she came back. In the meantime, I made a couple of phone calls to better clarify what was lacking in my paperwork.

When she came back, she said, "I'm not going to talk to anyone on the phone!"

"And I'm not going to make you either," I replied. I continued waiting while other people were getting their paperwork done.

The supervisor's assistant came by. "Get away!" she told me.

"But I'm waiting for—"

"GET AWAY FROM THE DOOR!" she yelled at me.

Silence. Everyone stopped what they were doing and turned to look at me.

"I'm waiting for the supervisor," I told her, hands shaking and palms sweating. My nerves had gotten the best of me, and as I waited to talk to the supervisor, I took the chance to compose myself. Then I firmly told the supervisor, "Ma'am, I feel like you're discriminating against me. I don't know why you're doing so, but you are. Kindly tell me what has to be done to get this paperwork over with."

"Bring a letter stating the reason why you need the old document changed," she said and walked away.

I walked towards the entrance and noticed two teenagers laughing away at the scene that had just taken place. I gave them a hard stare in the eyes and walked away. I decided to walk back to the supervisor just to make sure I had it all down.

"You're sure that a letter is all I need?" I asked.

"Yes," she said. I smiled and walked out the door.

"That lady sure is a you-know-what," a man came up and told me. "She did the same thing to me when I brought in my paperwork."

Sometimes even those who are supposed to help you will not; they won't care, just like that supervisor didn't care. Those man's words proved to me that the supervisor was like that with everyone. It didn't help that I accidentally walked in wearing flip-flops with my hair in a bun, looking extremely fatigued.

The next day, I was prepared. Everything went smoothly. The funniest part was that another man who was waiting in line next to me told me something interesting about this organization. "You know, even though I'm in a high position in another organization, I get no respect from these people over here. They treat everyone like dogs."

When he told me this, I realized that I was right in what I did the day before. I sat there, smiling, and as we shared our experiences with each other, I found out that everyone has their own fights. I'm happy to say that I got my paperwork done soon after. It turns out that the same lady ended up helping me without even realizing what had happened the day before. It's funny how things work out like that.

Learning when to fight is the most vital thing anyone will ever learn in his or her life. Learning when to fight and when to let go changes you. You become more balanced, and you learn how to be less defensive about every little thing.

The smaller things become insignificant as your mind learns to accept how the world is and how people are. Once you understand this, you're set for life. Life becomes easier for you and everything just magically appears to get better. Situations tend to work out in your favor, and people who weren't willing to help you at first actually start to help you without even being asked to. That's the beauty of knowing when to argue. You become the master of your world, and you gain control over your life. Isn't that what we all strive for?

5

Perfection in Imperfection

When I was a teenager, I was known to be a perfectionist. I would spend time organizing my books, CDs, and DVDs in alphabetical or numerical order. This would always relieve my stress from school and help me unwind every day. Along with that, I used to do a bit of meditation to help me sleep at night. Organizing things really aided me in becoming more disciplined, but at the same time, I felt that I wasted a lot of effort on things that didn't really matter. This would just put me further behind in completing the task at hand.

I use to be a procrastinator. Waiting until the last minute for school projects that had to be completed or studying for my exams the day before they took place was my forte. One night, as I was slogging away at a history paper, I ended up just calling it quits. I literally wrote as much as I could and then went to bed. It was 2 a.m. When I woke up at 6 a.m., my head was pounding. I really didn't like doing things at the last minute, especially since I always wanted every little detail to be perfect for whatever work I was submitting at school. But the amount of schoolwork would not permit me to continue being a perfectionist.

On the other hand, there were days when I would not allow myself to stop correcting my work until I thought it was the best it could possibly be. That was also a problem; a lot of time got wasted and school priorities weren't acknowledged during this process either. I understood that I could no longer keep pushing myself like this and staying awake late at night.

Soon, the most unimaginable thing happened; I almost passed out while I was running outside. I ran as I normally did around the park, but darkness suddenly gathered around me. My vision blackened, and I felt my knees buckle.

"STOP!" I yelled to my trainer.

She asked me, "What happened?"

"I don't know…" I mumbled meekly. I was befuddled and disoriented.

The next day, I went to the hospital. "Let me put on some music for you," the nurse said as the MRI machine whirred to life.

"Oh no…" I said out loud.

"It's okay," the nurse said. He put the headphones on me, and the MRI scan started.

The machine covering me gave me very little space to move; I felt claustrophobic. Tick-tock, tick-tock! "Oh no…" I said to myself. My breathing quickened, and my vision started to swirl. I was panicking.

"Please wait for the results," the nurse told my parents and me.

After what felt like an eternity, the nurse came back with the doctor. "Everything's fine," the doctor told us. I was relieved.

"I want to train indoors from now on," I told my personal trainer. We started doing some light workouts at home. The days passed by, and going outdoors started to become increasingly difficult for me.

"Want to go outside?" my parents would ask me.

"NO!" I would say.

A few MRI tests and a few days later, no answer could be found as to why I had almost passed out while running. All that we could decipher was that I was stressed, tired, and dehydrated. The workouts then became lighter, and we stopped going outside altogether.

This was a huge wake-up call for me. I had to stop making sure that everything was perfect and just accept the imperfection. After all, imperfection is what makes us human. Imperfection is what makes the world around us so beautiful.

The days went by, and I started to get panic attacks and developed a full-fledged fear of going outside. I also started to get dizzy spells from my panic attacks. Anytime anyone even mentioned going outside, even to the mall or to a café,

I would panic. I could already sense the swirling dizziness around me, and I would start to tremble at the thought of going outside. It got to the point where I could not even participate in my PE classes at school. I was filled with fear.

Every day at school was a huge hurdle for me to overcome. I struggled to go to my classes and tried to focus on my studies. I panicked as soon as lunchtime started. Whenever I had no choice but to sit outside, I would sit in the shade near the entrance and focus on eating. When I walked up the stairs in school, even if I was remotely scared, that fear transformed into a full-blown panic attack. I would start feeling dizzy, break into a cold sweat, and feel sick to my stomach.

"What am I going to do?" I thought out loud when I got home one day. I had suffered from multiple panic attacks.

Eventually, my energy dwindled, and I became a bit depressed. I discussed my problem with my grandmother, the doctor, and she said it was all in my mind. She encouraged me to move past my fear and go outside. I tried doing this step by step. I started with our backyard.

Our pug, Jewel, would run around in circles as I sat there watching him. He would then sit and stare right back at me, all tuckered out. If a pigeon came near him, he would start chasing it and running all over again.

Jewel wasn't always this energetic. When we first got him, he was scared of the vacuum cleaner, and extremely afraid of luggage. One time, he saw the vacuum cleaner being used, and he dashed in the other direction, yelping away. After some time though, he got over this fear.

From this little puppy, I learned how to get over my fear of going outside. When I saw him facing his fear of going near the vacuum cleaner, I knew I could also get over my irrational fear of going outside.

Soon, I started going to the mall again. I also started going out to meet my friends, and to eat outside. I was a bit wary at first, but I was able to build up my strength.

Later, while I was at a friend's house, I had the worst panic attack ever. What started out as a slight dizzy spell soon became a debilitating migraine in which my vision was affected. My friend's mother took me to the emergency room. The nurse checked my pulse, and then we met the doctor. Nothing was wrong with me; it was just a normal migraine.

My frequent panic attacks and migraines were draining my energy and making me feel so hopeless about everything. As I grew more depressed, my thoughts became increasingly dark, and my outlook on life became more negative. I became a non-believer in everything I held dear and grew more and more tired of life. Since I forced myself to get up every day to go to school and study, I would go to sleep extremely early. I just didn't have the strength to stay awake past 8:30 p.m.

One day, I heard back from a college I had applied to. I opened the letter slowly. It said, "We regret to inform you that we have declined your application to our university…."

"NO!" I yelled.

"It's okay," my parents said.

That night was the lowest point in my life. My mind was clouded with emotions and panic. I grabbed a razor blade and lightly cut my skin, literally making just a few tiny scratches. Panicking even more, I ran, crying hysterically, to my parents' room. My sister was asleep in the room next to me but did not hear me crying.

"Open the door!" I told my parents.

My mother saw me. "Are you alright?" she asked, concerned.

"I need to talk to you!" I told her. My dad also got up to listen. "I took a blade…and I cut my skin. It's a superficial cut, but I only did it because I'm upset!" I sobbed.

"Look, I understand what happened, but why did you do such a thing?" my mother asked me calmly.

"I didn't get into the university I wanted! I'M A FAILURE! EVERYONE WILL NOW KNOW I AM A FAILURE!!!" I cried away, soaking my PJs with tears. I was being a bit melodramatic and trying to get attention. I was a real attention-seeker as a teenager.

"Don't worry," my mother said. "Please promise me you won't do such a thing to yourself again. We all love you. You sure you're okay? Because this seems like you're just trying to get our attention."

"Yes, I was," I told her. "I had no other intention."

The next day, I spoke to my grandmother, the doctor. "You sure you don't want to speak to a therapist?" she asked. "I can help you, but you have to listen to me."

I did listen to her; I wanted to get past feeling low. I was emotionally disturbed due to my panic attacks. Once I understood why they were happening, I also understood why I was feeling emotionally low. I promised to never let myself get to that point again or do anything silly for attention, since I do care a lot about my health and well-being. It was also really immature of me because I did not think about how my loved ones would feel about my predicament. I learned how to appreciate myself after everything that happened.

My panic attacks were prompted by anxiety and my fear of going outside. After I had almost passed out while running, my mind was fixated on believing that going outside was bad. I had to un-train myself and learn how to go outside without panicking and wasting my energy on thinking about whether I was going to panic or not.

My mother was also very understanding of the situation I was in. She told me that because of all of the stress from bullies and because of my recent traumatizing experience in which I had almost passed out while running, I had created this new fear. I started to do some meditation with her, and she started to become an unexpected mentor for me. Whatever problem came my way, she was there to help me along. She believed that I would get past this problem, and she was right. I soon got over this hindrance. My panic attacks decreased, and my dizzy spells stopped completely.

Soon my high school graduation day came, and as I sang on stage with a select few backup singers in the choir, something dawned upon me. I was so happy that my high school years were now behind me and that I was never going to see these people again. My heart was brimming with joy. Words could not describe the utter peace I found within myself right then. It was at that moment that I chose to stop being a perfectionist and start anew. I chose to be a blend of perfection and imperfection.

Initially, I still had a few panic attacks and some dizzy spells at college, but I was able to overcome that as well. I strongly believed that I could get rid of my irrational fear of going outside, and I did.

Thus, I allowed myself to perfect certain issues that I came across, but more so when it came to college work. Otherwise, I was the perfect imperfectionist. I always loved a good mistake. Mistakes are the greatest lessons in life. Plus, it's nice to know that I am not under that much pressure to be the perfect person or to submit the perfect school project. Some of my best projects were the ones that I didn't put much effort into—the ones where I just went with the flow.

People have their nervous tics. Mine just happens to be scratching. My skin will get easily irritated, burst into hives and feel really itchy whenever I get a bit tense. Or I'll get a patch of eczema. Skin picking is a strange habit.

When I was about seven in Mumbai, I saw something quite disturbing. I noticed my friend casually picking away at a scab on her knee, and then peeling it off. Curious to know what that felt like, I started doing it too.

At the time, I was dealing with bullies and only had a couple of friends. Every time anyone would bully me, I would scratch like crazy. Bullying was a trigger for me. Scratching became an outlet and refuge from the bullying, and soon enough, my skin started getting really bad.

"Okay, let's put up a chart and see if you can stop scratching," my mother said. "You get a reward if you don't scratch!" The red and white chart was hung up near the bathroom in the room that I shared with my sister.

"Stop scratching!" my sister would always tell me whenever she saw me scratching away. She would get really annoyed at this habit of mine.

The years passed by with this on-and-off habit, and I would spend hours in the bathroom, engrossed in my scratching fits. I would feel upset and moody about it later on, but as soon as the feeling was gone, I would start again. I would feel really low and sorry for myself, and that just made things worse.

When I became a teenager, this habit did slow down a bit, but then became worse. Whenever anything bad happened in my life, I would resort to scratching in various different ways. When I became an adult, I would conceal this anxious habit as I was embarrassed about how awful it was. I would hide in the bathroom and pick at my skin. I would even scratch in plain sight, hiding my hands under my desk.

Having eczema didn't help either although I was unaware that I had eczema until a few years ago. Eczema caused my skin to become really scaly and itchy due to the stress I had.

Bad grades in college? Scratch. Bullies? Scratch. Argument with my parents? Scratch. Before I got married, I managed to stop, but as soon as that was over, I reverted back to this habit. It was like an addiction I couldn't get rid of. My husband knew that I had a problem, but even he could not stop me from damaging my skin. I disliked the fact that my scratching was lowering my self-esteem (who likes walking around with discolored or scaly skin anyways?)

Sleepless nights ensued, and this took a toll on my emotional health. I decided to get help from a life coach who also happened to be a dear friend of mine.

"You know you're only scratching because it's a habit that you picked up early on in your life. Whenever something triggers your emotions, you scratch. It's also why you always feel itchy whenever a stressful situation comes up."

I also sought advice from my grandmother, the doctor. "Start thinking before you scratch," she said. "Think about how you are feeling now and why you are feeling that way."

I knew that I couldn't continue scratching every time I got nervous. I wanted to be confident, and this habit was stopping me from reaching my full potential. Before I became thirty, this habit finally slowed down. Every time I feel the anxious urge to scratch, I first think of why I want to do so.

I know it's all in my head, and I have to unlearn this behavior. I know I'll be rid of this shortcoming soon enough. As it is, I don't drink, smoke, party hard, stay up really late, or skip work regularly. I'm also an eggetarian for health reasons and I eat reasonably healthy food (plus the occasional chocolate bar or fries). I'm quite disciplined, aside from the fact that I'm a perfectionist, have a bit of a short temper (I'm a sensitive soul), and tend to feel itchy when under a lot of stress.

Yet, I'm also fortunate enough that none of these three issues affect my work. I make sure to focus only on work when I am working and not on anything else. These problems also don't influence the way I am as a person or my perspective on life (I like to think of myself as a logical optimist who looks at things in the most realistically positive way possible).

When I'm in my perfectionist mode, I use that to my advantage to motivate myself to get things done. I also use that to organize my home, office, and other projects. It also ensures that I put my best foot forward when it comes to getting things done.

When I feel angry, I use that as a catalyst to propel me toward change. It also helps me to move ahead in my life and address issues that are important to me. At times, I might burst into a fit of anger, but that rarely happens (let's say once in a while and only if someone or something has really pushed my buttons). I do get irritated about certain problems, but I calm down fairly quickly, although I tend to say some fairly offensive things at the time.

When it comes to scratching, I've learned to think twice before acting out. It's made me more mindful, and I care even more about how I am right now. It also made me realize that I don't like having such distasteful habits as they are not good for me in the long run. I would not like to have gruesome marks all over my skin for no reason. It also makes me feel a bit insecure even when I'm usually fairly confident.

Scratching doesn't define me as a person; it is not the way I am. If I could have stopped this silly habit before, I would have. Skin-picking lowers my self-esteem, makes me lose sleep, makes me feel edgy, and wastes my time. This habit comes in the way of whatever else I could have been doing.

They say that time heals everything, and letting go of my imperfections will help me get past the skin-picking. The life-coaching sessions and my mindfulness exercises, such as meditation, have helped reduce my scratching tremendously. Habits shouldn't define you; you should define yourself.

Imperfections can be used to balance your life and to get ahead of the little obstacles that may come your way. That's the true power of perfection in imperfection. Once you learn to harness this, you can achieve anything that your heart desires. That's how I was able to move up the corporate ladder so quickly; I used my flaws as my strengths to become the businesswoman that I am today.

6

Keep Going

Life isn't always rosy, and rarely does it go the way it's supposed to. September 11th, 2001. The attacks had just happened in New York, while many of my friends and family members were nearby. My immediate family had just moved to Dubai a month ago, and we were shaken. My mother switched on the TV and saw it happening. My sister and I came back from school. We stared at the TV in shock.

"This isn't a movie, kids," my mother told us, crying. She called our family in the States. "It'll be okay," she told her mother as tears streamed down her face. I could hear my grandmother crying away on the phone while I sat there silently.

The next day, school was cancelled. We sat at home, petrified about the events that had transpired the day before. I couldn't stomach what had happened and my sister was too young to understand it fully. All she knew was that something bad had happened, and everyone was crying.

I couldn't sleep for the next few days; my sister and I slept on the floor in our parents' room. We were both too scared to sleep alone for the next few months. I kept having nightmares of the towers falling and burning while people jumped out. I just couldn't fathom what had happened. For a kid, it was too much to handle.

Several years later, while I was in college, the Mumbai attacks happened. November 26th, 2008. Mumbai was under attack. Two prominent hotels and a few other places had been targeted. Those two hotels were the ones that most of my friends and family members usually went to. In fact, my parents went to one of those places every week for dinner. That day, however, my father was busy with work, and my mother didn't want to go on her own. Two of my friends, who also worked at one of those hotels, had taken the day off.

Although my near and dear ones were lucky, many others were not. A lot of our friends lost people they knew. I had just come home from college to my grandmother's house. The news was on. I couldn't believe what was happening. I immediately called my parents. I then called my two friends who worked at the hotel to make sure that they were okay.

Afterwards, I messaged everyone I knew who stayed in Mumbai. Most of my friends had come home after work or college, and I was relieved to know that they were alright. But the fact that my parents could have been there shook me to the core. From that day on, I became closer to my parents. I learned not to take them or anyone else for granted.

When the hotel finally reopened, my parents were invited. They were busy that day and did not go, but we all went there a few days after the official reopening. As I walked through the hotel lobby, I kept imagining what had happened just a year ago. The screams, the massacre, and the blood still flowed through my mind just as I had seen it on TV a year ago. It troubled me deeply.

"I can't eat here again," I told my parents.

A few years later, I managed to build up the strength to go there and eat at one of the restaurants that was attacked. I still felt disturbed by what had happened; many people who used to work there were no more. Almost ten years later, I am finally able to go and eat there without feeling upset. I remind myself that life goes on, and we can't stop living just because something terrible happened. We have to accept what has happened, become stronger, and push onwards. That's the only way we can really live our lives after something so horrible happens.

Random incidents also happen. I happened to be in a really bad car crash when I was twelve. The car was totaled, my chauffer was bleeding from his nose, and my sister and I had slight bruises on our hands and faces. We were on the way to school, as usual. That day, we were running late because our usual car was blocked by another car in the garage. We ended up taking another car and left.

My sister and I were listening to our favorite song on repeat as we usually did; we were excited to go meet our friends at school. We were on the highway when, out of the blue, an orange truck came crashing into us from the side. Our whole car was totaled. Blood splattered on my chauffer, and I saw my sister shaking and howling away. I was in shock. By then, the truck driver was long gone.

"His red eyes," my chauffeur told me in Hindi, wiping away the blood from his nose. "I think he was drunk..."

As he cleaned himself up, we got out of the car and waited for someone to come by. At that time, we didn't have personal cell phones, and we had to patiently wait for help. A car stopped. It was one of the students and his mother on the way to our school.

"My goodness, what happened? Are you all okay?" my schoolmate's mother asked.

My chauffeur, my sister, and I were still in shock, but I managed to say "Thank you..." softly to her.

When we reached the school, my classmates were running around the track for PE. One of my classmates stopped in her tracks. She looked at us, very disheartened and confused. She then went back to running. The five of us continued walking and went to the nurse.

"You are all very lucky. Your chauffeur just has some slight bleeding, but it should subside soon." Then, the nurse called my mother.

One of our relatives came to pick us up along with her. "My darlings, you'll be okay!" my relative said as she hugged my sister and me.

We called our family doctor at home, and she examined everyone. "Your chauffeur will be okay. He just has an external injury. As for your kids, they just have some bruising. That will go away. They are all still shaking because of the shock, but they will be fine soon."

Years later, I was preparing to get my driver's license. That was a task indeed for me. I was still scared of any truck that would come near my car. I soon became petrified of driving on the highway. "You have to learn to drive everywhere," my driving instructor would say. He would tell me to go on the highway every time we had a lesson, even if I was reluctant, in order to get over my fear.

The first time I went on the highway was really bad. I kept breaking and veering all over the place. "You've got to hit the brakes only when you're getting too close to the car in front," he said. After that ordeal was over, I was glad to go home. Day after day, week after week, my driving instructor would constantly take me back to the main highway and make me drive. After a while, I became confident. I passed my driving test on the first try.

A few days later, when I went on my own on the highway, my irrational fear of trucks came back. I would watch these large freight trucks passing near me, and I would instantly panic. Eventually, I overcame this, or so I thought.

One day, when we were on our way back after a family event, it was dark and foggy outside.

"Oh no, there's way too much fog!" I told everyone. I almost missed the exit and accidentally got stuck near the exit line. Cars were passing by on both sides of the highway, and I was shaking.

"What are you doing? GO!!!!" my grandmother yelled.

"JUST DRIVE!" my sister screamed.

Everyone in the car was panicking. I finally got off that point and re-exited the highway.

A few years later, I was driving on the highway with my family in the car again. Orange cones shone ahead in the dark, and I swerved to the side. BEEEP BEEEPPPPP!!!!! A large truck was trying to get by; it was already halfway in my lane. I skidded to the side and went back to my original lane.

"That was unbelievable!" my uncle said.

"You can't let anyone bully you," my grandmother said.

"Sorry guys!" I told them.

The next time, I was much more mindful of what was happening on the road and not focused on what everyone was talking about in the car.

Personal loss is unavoidable. A couple of months ago, I lost someone very close to my heart; my grandaunt. She was battling with an autoimmune disease and passed away in the middle of the night in the United States. It was about 7 a.m. in Dubai when my phone rang.

"She's gone…" my mother sobbed.

Tears welled up in my eyes, and I started crying uncontrollably. My husband comforted me as I sat in bed, crying away. I took the next flight out and attended my grandaunt's funeral the day after.

My grandaunt wasn't just another relative to me. She would always stop by my grandmother's house in the U.S. to visit all of us while my mother and I attended our classes in New York. She would bring us sweets or home-cooked food, and she always remembered our birthdays. She was the sweetest woman I knew and one of the strongest.

The day I found out that she had a terrible autoimmune disease, I knew she would fight until the very end. And she did. Whenever I got the chance, I would stop by the hospital and visit her. Although she was terribly weak, her face would always light up whenever she saw me. She would start talking to me, asking how my CIBE certification was going.

"Let's celebrate once you graduate!" she would tell me. "I want to have a party for you."

She really believed that she would be around until then. I loved her fighting spirit. She was very proud of the woman I was. I was proud of her too. She was such a humble woman and loved her family to bits. She cared more about how we felt at that moment than herself!

"I got you some homemade food. It's your favorite!" I would tell her each time I went to see her.

Exhausted as she was, she would pick up the box of food and start eating. My grandmother would be there at her side just in case, but my grandaunt refused her help.

"Thank you, but I can eat on my own," she would say.

We watched this petite woman happily munching away on her food. It was like watching a little kid eat candy.

My grandaunt soon got discharged from the hospital and started staying at her house again. Our family continued to visit her at home.

One day, she burst into tears. "I don't know if I can do this!" she cried.

My sister and I consoled her. "You're okay!" I told her comfortingly, "You'll be fine soon."

She stopped crying then. My grandaunt soon starting talking more and more to us all; she would spend her time watching TV and looking forward to our visits.

Just before I left to return to Dubai, I met her one last time. I still remember that I was scratching away at the eczema on my hands, since it was cold outside. I looked at her and saw the sadness in her eyes.

"I love you," I told her and gave her a hug.

A few weeks later, she passed away at home in her sleep.

People like my grandaunt are the bravest. She gave us hope that anyone can face anything as long as they believe that they can. Nothing can stop them from living. She was kind-hearted and helpful. She only saw the goodness in everyone.

When she passed on, I knew her life was not lived in vain. She taught my family and me to be resilient.

My great-grandmother was another loved one whom I lost a few years ago. My husband and I were fortunate enough to meet her right after we got engaged.

The week before she passed away, I met her in Mumbai. I was at work that day and had this strange feeling inside me that told me to go meet her. I called her after work and stopped by. She was so happy to see me, and we started talking about my wedding plans.

A week or so later, she passed away due to a heart attack at home; she was around ninety-three years old.

This woman was my idol. She was able to live normally and do whatever she wanted on her own until her last breath. She was a classy lady who stood her ground. Although she was not well-educated, she accomplished many feats.

She was a freedom fighter in India's fight for independence from Britain. She got married when she was still a teenager and had her first child when she was eighteen. She had three kids who are all well-educated, although she lost her husband the year I was born and dealt with that. She travelled between the United States and India every year. She managed her own household and was fiercely independent. She would only ask for help when absolutely necessary. She was also very frank and opinionated, just like me.

When I started going to college, my great-grandmother was the first one to support me. She was proud of what I was doing. She even attended my graduation at Drexel. When I started working, she cheered me on. When I started my MBA, she couldn't have been happier.

But whenever I did something wrong, my great-grandmother would be the first person to tell me so, quite directly. She didn't hold back, and we didn't mind it when she expressed her opinions freely.

"Is that shirt supposed to be off-the-shoulder?" she asked me in Sindhi when I came back one day from college.

My grandmother chimed in, "Yes, it's a style nowadays."

"Ah, I see," my great-grandmother replied. She was very accepting of the way things were.

We use to travel together from India to the U.S. My great-grandmother would watch some movies and then get bored during the flight. She would then turn towards me to talk. As soon as our eyes met, we would burst out laughing. Even when we got home, she would look at me and burst out laughing. I don't know why we used to laugh every time we were bored or out of things to talk about, but it was an understanding that we had. It's like we knew something others didn't.

My great-grandmother became a source of help and inspiration to my family. She was one brilliant woman I won't forget.

My great-grandmother was also a brilliant cook. She used to make wonderful *mithai* (Indian sweets) for my entire family, especially me. I would always be the first one to try out whatever she had made that day, and she would make something extra just for me. Whenever I came to my grandmother's house on the weekends, she would keep some food ready for me.

The day she passed away, I was in Dubai. Circumstances at the time did not permit me to attend her funeral, and I was deeply saddened by this.

That year was one of the saddest years of my life. I always felt like she was still there when I went to Mumbai or visited her room in my grandmother's house. My family and I took time to really process the fact that she was no more.

I will always remember her fondly as a wonderful woman who was the greatest person in my life. After all, she was the one who inspired me to be who I am.

Other losses can happen too, like that of my pug, Jewel. Pets become a part of the family very quickly, but don't live as long. Jewel was a gem in our family. He was the sweetest little pug that we could ask for. He came to us in Dubai and passed away in Mumbai. He was fourteen when he passed on.

The last few months of his life were very painful. His health started to suddenly deteriorate. His kidneys started to fail and there was no option remaining except to put him to sleep. Still, it was a hard decision for us to make.

When we first got Jewel, he was this tiny little pup with a bright pink nose. The breeder had brought him to our home. Jewel ran up to me.

"He smells like strawberries," I told my family.

He then pooped near the front door in excitement. "I'll clean it!" I happily told my parents.

My mother was frightened of dogs, yet she made an exception for my sister who had always wanted one.

"I have no friends here, so I want a dog!" she would say to my parents. Jewel was the answer.

My mother would avoid being around Jewel, and Jewel would do the same. Once, my mother happened to be walking downstairs, and Jewel was out and about, running around in the foyer. My mother froze when she saw the puppy. Jewel stopped in his tracks too and then ran the other way.

My mother soon realized that Jewel knew that she was scared of him. That was why he did not come up to her, even if he was moving around the place.

A couple of years later, when my sister got Charlie Brown, a Yorkshire terrier, my mother started to warm up to dogs. She started petting Jewel, and Jewel grew closer to her. The day that Jewel got sick was the saddest day of my mother's life. My mother loved Jewel the most since he was the first dog that we had.

The day that I flew from Dubai to Mumbai, I could only think of my dear Jewel, crying and suffering at the veterinary hospital.

The next day, I saw him. He was a scrawny little thing, but he was full of life. His eyes lit up like a puppy's as he saw my parents and me surrounding him. He was so active that the vet was shocked. He had even eaten food before we got there.

As the vet broke the news to us that Jewel was dying, we

started to tear up.

"Please be strong for Jewel," the vet said. "You must not cry in front of him."

We swallowed our sadness and all three of us put on a brave face.

The vet went out of the room as we spent our last few precious moments with Jewel. Another vet came in. He explained what was going to be done, and we all asked him if we could be there while Jewel was being put to sleep. We waited in silence around Jewel, putting on our bravest faces in order to comfort him.

"It'll be okay," we all told him.

Jewel realized what the vet was doing and kicked him.

"It's going to be okay, Jewel," I told him, trying my best to hold back my tears.

A few minutes later, he was gone. His eyes were wide open, and he looked like he was just relaxing. The body was then taken away, and my parents and I started crying uncontrollably.

My father told us, "Jewel was strong till the end. As soon as I told him that you guys were coming, he started to act normally. That's why he ate his food today."

We can all learn from our pets. Jewel was a fighter who stayed extremely relaxed until the end. We should all have that calmness in our lives, no matter how bad the situation is.

Shefali Karani

Unforeseen circumstances and personal loss can affect our lives immensely. Once we learn how to deal with these situations, we also learn how to better handle life. We learn how to balance our lives and move ahead by focusing on the moment. We also learn that the right thing in such a situation is to remain calm and composed. We also learn never to take anything for granted. That is the greatest lesson of all.

7

Using Anger as a Tool

Anger is passion. I'm very passionate about everything I do, and hence, I am also prone to being quite short-tempered. When I was a teenager, I did not use my anger wisely, but I now know how to use anger to my advantage. Whenever I feel any sort of anger bubbling up inside, I use it as a force for change as well as a force for good.

When I got married, I had to move from India to Dubai again. This meant that my work had to be done remotely from Dubai as my main office was in Mumbai, India. This also meant that I had to be very flexible in terms of work timings and where I chose to work from.

I tried setting up an actual office in Dubai, but to no avail. It just wasn't feasible, no matter how I looked at my work situation.

Things started looking bleak for me, and, as I tried working from my husband's house, a café, and even my parents' house in Dubai, I grew even more weary. How was I going to handle my work from Dubai? Soon, I actually grew a bit angry at the situation I was in, but I chose to use that anger to find a solution.

I really couldn't work from my husband's house as there were too many distractions. Plus, I felt really uncomfortable having to work from home. It made me feel even worse, and I was extremely hopeless about getting any actual work done. The ambience didn't really feel like an office to me, so I decided to eliminate that option after a while.

I even tried working from my laptop at a café once, but that was no good at all! I was so distracted with all the commotion around me that I couldn't really work properly. That choice was eventually dropped from my list of places to work from.

A couple of months later, I decided to work from my parents' house in Dubai. Since they were never really around, I used that as an opportunity to form a home office for myself, with their permission and support.

Most major meetings were held in Mumbai, and I travelled for those whenever necessary. It was a short flight from Dubai to Mumbai, which made it convenient for me. The rest of the meetings were held at my home office in Dubai or a place nearby.

Once I decided to do this, my anger disappeared. I became even more motivated to work properly from my home office. I literally converted one of the rooms my parents had for me into an office space. No one really disturbs me while I work, since my mother is normally working from her home office as well. I can now focus in that space for as long as I like.

Soon enough, another problem arose. I couldn't work during

normal office timings in Mumbai as there was a slight time difference in Dubai. Plus, workdays in Dubai are different from workdays in Mumbai. I had to work from Saturday to Thursday in Dubai, with Friday off, as was the norm here. In Mumbai, the office worked from Monday to Friday, and sometimes on Saturday too. Sunday was the day off in India.

Initially, I was a bit frustrated and angry that I couldn't keep up with the companies' work in India. It was then that I decided that perhaps I needed to acknowledge the fact that I couldn't work full-time like I used to in Mumbai.

Now I work part-time from my home office in Dubai and full-time whenever I am at the office in Mumbai. This works out well for me, and as I learned to change my approach to the situation I was in, things changed for me. I actually got promoted to a board director some time ago, and am now able to keep up with whatever tasks I have at hand. Having a fixed daily schedule works too.

I created a schedule in which I go to the gym in the morning near my home office, go to work soon after, eat lunch, freshen up, and then start working until the time I go back to my husband's house in the evening.

At first, I was a bit upset and angry about not having a normal work schedule, but my parents helped me understand that it just wasn't possible. Even my mother has a similar work routine, and she's fine with the way things are. She is a board director too.

I realized then that I was scared that people wouldn't take me seriously because I was working remotely from a home office. But it was the opposite instead! People respect me a lot more now because I get my work done, and I attend most of our major meetings in Mumbai. My promotion only happened after I got my home office routine in order.

Sometimes, the occasional social event would come up for a friend or a relative, and there were also outings with my mother or husband. But, I just reminded myself that I had to balance it all out. I can't just focus on work and forget about everything else. That would also create anger within myself. I had to take a break once in a while.

It's important to allow yourself to fulfil certain family and social obligations as well in order to live a well-balanced life. After a while, I transformed into a quiet social butterfly that attended such events whenever necessary. I also maintained my status of being a well-seasoned executive at work.

Anger is a force that helped me develop my career even more; because of my anger and frustration, I was able to create a good routine for myself while working remotely from my home office in Dubai. Anger also helped me focus on my work in ways that I could not even imagine were possible.

"I love you!" my sister cried while hugging me during my wedding. My younger sister and I didn't always get along. We use to fight and argue every chance we got. As kids and teenagers, we were very different from each other. Even though there was just a three-year age gap between us, our personalities differed vastly.

When we were kids, I would take her toys and replace them with my broken ones. Whenever our friends came over, I would shut the room door on her. She would sit outside, waiting for one of my friends to reopen the door. I would blame her for every little mistake, even if I was the one who was responsible.

My sister had the utmost patience with me. Even when I yelled, screamed, and threw temper tantrums, she would just sit quietly, taking it all in. I was a total tomboy then.

But once we became teenagers, it was different. My sister would yell back and argue with me. She would shut the door on me whenever her friends came over and exclude me from everything possible. She would also call me fat since I was overweight then. She kept poking fun at whatever I did in front of others. My sister loved me but she wanted to show me that she didn't like the way I had yelled at her when I was younger.

I was also one pretty angry teenager. I would argue with my parents about everything under the sun: my clothes, going out with boys (I was not allowed to do so, and I'm glad that I didn't go out with anyone in school), going to parties, and going shopping.

I liked dressing up in logo t-shirts (as was all the rage at that time), cargo pants, and colorful skirts. But our school in Dubai had uniforms, just like most private schools did. So, clothing became a form of rebellion for me.

Whenever I could dress up at home, I would wear logo shirts that had funny sayings on them, shiny tank tops, etc.

My parents weren't always happy with the clothes I wore. My mother wanted me to look more girly, but my dad didn't really say much about this issue.

Being overweight, I had a huge stomach that made me look really bad.

"You can't eat that!" my mother would yell at me.

She was concerned as I was shorter than her at the time and looked very unhealthy. She took me to a nutritionist, but that didn't help much. I started to secretly eat food behind her back (I didn't consider soup and salad a proper dinner). I would get my chauffeur to bring back food and drinks for me from outside the house and eat away while watching TV. This wasn't a good idea because I soon got mad at others for teasing me about my weight.

People would call me baby elephant, fatty, or just plain ugly because I had such a big tummy.

"I'm no baby elephant! I'm like the actress that you just saw," I would tell my friend angrily.

The day I realized I had had enough of the teasing was the day I started working out. I also grew a few more inches in height once I started going to college and was then taller than my mother. My sister is still much taller and skinnier than me today, but at least I look normal and am fit. My anger disappeared once I learned to take care of myself.

I would still argue away with my sister when I started college as she had more friends than I did. She was skinny and tall as well as smart and more sociable than me. I envied her life.

I would get easily irritated with her due to my insecurities.

But during my last year of college, she got into the same college as me, and we decided to live together. We got a nice apartment on campus, and we took turns cleaning it. It was then that we learned to accept the way we were. I learned to tolerate her little quirks, and she learned to tolerate my pet peeves. We both understood why we were fighting; we didn't really know ourselves until then, and our different personalities tore us apart. Once we accepted that fact, we grew close.

Soon, we started sharing secrets with each other; and her friends became my friends and vice versa. We would go out of our way to help each other if either of us was unwell or feeling low. She would even cover up for me if I had done something wrong by mistake or had forgotten to call my parents. My sister became my best friend, and we both realized how similar we really were. The day I graduated, my sister was so happy for me that she could not stop telling me how proud she was to have me as a big sister.

Nowadays, she stays in New York while I'm mostly in Dubai. I hardly get to see her, but whenever I do, we act as if we haven't seen each other in years! We keep in touch and call each other on the phone. We still act like two very different people, but, at times, people think we are twins! That happens because we both dress alike and look quite similar, other than the fact that she's a good three inches taller than me and much more slender.

Although she has a career as an associate fashion editor for a well-known online publication and I'm an executive working with my family, we both have similar goals in our lives. We both want to be the best that we can be, no matter what, despite the occasional tiffs that we have.

Cookie, my rescue dog, also had a lot of anger issues. When my parents first got Cookie in Dubai, he was this little angry puppy who wanted to bite any time he got scared of anyone or anything. He was an out-of-control canine who was quite moody. My family and I understood that it was possibly because of what he had gone through, since he had a slightly twisted front paw. He still ran like the wind and was very loving whenever he was calm.

When I first met Cookie, he was this scrawny little pup with a whole bunch of maladies. The moment Cookie saw me, he ran up to me and wanted to sit with me. As he crawled into my lap, he stared into my eyes. The way he looked at me was so heartfelt; I could see the love in his eyes. He raised his nose to touch my chin, and he then sat back down, relaxed.

"He connected with you!" my friend said.

"Yes, he seems very loving," I said.

We started introducing Cookie slowly to our family and house. We had to be sure he was comfortable.

The first day he came to our house, he ran and growled at the help. He then tried snapping at them. He was a bit confused about who they were. Whenever one of my maids would open the door, he would growl and start jumping on the sofa.

I would have to hold him back. His anger was unexpected.

With some help and advice, I learned to understand that he was being protective, and he was acting out of fear. This was a new home for him, with new people. Of course, he wasn't going to get along with them right away. That's also why he was easily spooked whenever anyone had anything in their hands, even if it was food for him. He was quite silly, but the moment he calmed down, we could all see he was just trying to look out for himself.

The day my husband met Cookie was funny. Cookie was extremely happy to meet someone new who would give him lovely belly rubs.

"Can you please get my gym bag from upstairs?" I asked my husband.

With the bag in hand, my husband walked down the stairs. Immediately, Cookie became alert. "WOOF!!! WOOF!!! GRRR!!!"

"Ow!" my husband half-laughed and almost fell. Cookie had nipped him on the ankle.

The next day, when my husband came back, Cookie acted normal around him. But as soon as he went outside while Cookie was taking a walk with the help, Cookie started growling at him in the dark.

"Ha-ha!" I laughed.

Cookie continued getting mad at the people at home. So, we decided to get some help. We got some advice, and soon after, Cookie started to become calmer.

The reason Cookie was so angry all the time was because everyone at home was so angry or frustrated. The moment we all decided to calm down, Cookie started listening to us. As soon as he wanted to bite someone or something, we told him off. He listened. Cookie's anger soon reduced as we became calmer around him.

Soon, Cookie simmered down, and now he rarely gets mad when things don't go his way. Granted, Cookie is just a dog, but he taught me so much! I learned to be calmer around him. In fact, I learned to be calm wherever I went. His anger made me realize that I can't get mad at every little thing, especially when something doesn't go my way.

You have to be calm, composed and balanced from within, otherwise you'll soon feel like everything is going wrong! You also learn to make better decisions by being calm. I can already see that Cookie is making better decisions for himself by not getting so mad at everyone anymore. He's quite chilled out now.

Passionate anger can be good for you. If you know how to use it to change and balance your emotions, you can learn to focus on what exactly your anger is trying to tell you. When I was angry about my work situation, I used that anger to see what was really bothering me and then created an ideal work situation for myself. Not only that, but my anger went away once I knew the reason why I was truly angry.

When Cookie used to get really mad, I would observe him. When I realized what was really bothering him and asked for some help, Cookie soon calmed down. Nowadays, he hardly gets as upset as he used to.

Anger is a source of goodness if you can see the positivity in it. When you accept what your anger is trying to point out in your life, you can change the situation that you are in. Once you do that, things will start working out for you, and the smaller issues in your life won't frustrate you as much. You'll become a much more balanced and calmer person. That's how I am today.

8

Helping Others

Being a businesswoman, philanthropist, and muse has its perks. At the same time, it also comes with a lot of responsibility. Not only do I have to be a good role model for others around me but it is also expected that I should give back to society. As a high society person, I have always believed that it is my duty to help others in need as much as possible. I've done so in various ways over the years and have seen the difference it has made for others as well.

While I was still working on my Bachelor's degree in Philadelphia, a mentor from my school approached my family and me about a student in need. My family and I agreed to help fund that student anonymously.

One day, while I was at class, my mother called me. Our mentor had asked to meet us again that day. When we met her, she said that the student requested to meet the person who had provided his scholarship; he wished to thank them in person.

There I was, meeting this student who was almost the same age as me; he was shocked to see that such a young person had helped him out. Humbled by this, I told him that I was almost done with my Bachelor's degree and that my parents were the ones to thank, not me. From then on, I try and give whatever I can back to my alma mater. Little acts of help can make a huge difference!

During my MBA, a friend of mine was struggling to finish his last few months at college. He had no money to pay for his degree, and he asked everyone he knew for help. I decided to call him up and see how he was doing. It turned out that he was going to drop out of college since he had no money left to pay for his degree. He had completed more than half of the program there.

I told him, "Listen, I know someone who can help. How much do you need?"

I then called my parents and said, "A friend of mine is going to drop out of college if he can't pay for the program that he's in. He's almost done with his degree as well. Can I help him?"

My parents, of course, agreed, and soon, I paid off the amount my friend owed by giving it directly to the college.

My friend called and asked me, "Who was generous enough to do this? Please let me pay them back once I'm done with the program."

"My family and I did," I said, "And there's no need to pay

us back. The fact that you're getting your degree is enough for us."

Silence. "Wow! You guys are the greatest…Thank you, thank you!!" he sobbed on the phone.

We met up a few months later, and he thanked me again. Now, he has his degree and a stable job along with it.

While I was an undergraduate, I didn't always have money to give to others. So, I volunteered with an academic group at a food bank. We packed boxes of food for Thanksgiving, and the organization gave that food to people in need. I also used to go to an animal shelter and help around over there with the same academic group. After I finished my work there, I would always give a few dollars for the betterment of the shelter.

It was during this time that I became a writing tutor at my college. I would help correct other students' papers. It was the first job that I had and the hardest. I worked long hours, some of which were in-between classes. Working a job and maintaining my academic standing in the Honors Program was a task indeed, yet I did it with ease. When my assignment came to an end, I donated all the money I had made.

I learned the value of money when I had to work for it. That's why I knew I had enough, with or without this job.

A year after I graduated with my Bachelor's degree, a professor reached out to me. She asked me to be present during the students' career presentations. I was thrilled at the opportunity handed to me. I wore a beautiful dress and took my newly printed business cards with me.

"Hello, nice to meet you," I said as I met some of the other people there who were also helping out. I handed my business cards to them, and noticed their expressions change. Most of them were intimidated by such a young woman who was already an executive, especially a woman who belonged to a minority group. They all huddled together to talk, and I went inside the classroom.

The students were preparing for their presentations. A young girl came to the front of the class, her eyes darting around the room. Her voice was shaky when she began her presentation. As the presentation progressed, her voice became softer and softer, and she started to look at the ground. I kept looking at her, trying to figure out what was wrong.

When she finished, everyone applauded. None of the others who were there gave any sort of feedback to her.

"Look, you had a very nice presentation," I said, voice booming. Everyone turned to look at me. "But I think it could have been much better. You need to be confident and speak loudly! If you can't do that, then you won't get the job you like."

"Thank you for letting me know. I will definitely follow your advice!" the student said. She then went back to her seat.

After class, another student approached me. "Love your outfit!" she told me.

"Why, thank you!" I said.

"You know, I don't know how you did it, but you're an amazing woman! How did you accomplish so much so quickly?" she asked.

"When you have support from your family, you can do anything you set your mind to," I said.

"Wow! It was wonderful meeting you," she said and walked off.

When students come up to me and tell me such things, I know that I have accomplished something and made a difference.

Recently, I got the chance to mentor some students at Drexel. I was thrilled to have such an opportunity to share my experiences as a leader. That day, a student came up to me. "You truly have it all! You're rich, successful, and an Ivy League graduate. Amazing!"

I started sharing my experience at the school and what I had been doing after that. I also gave some invaluable advice to the students that I met. I even bumped into one of my former classmates who was also mentoring students that day.

After the program, I tried mingling with some of the other mentors. Some were nice, and some just ignored me. As I tried to talk to them, I realized it was of no use. I had intimidated them once again as I had done years ago with another group of mentors. This was plain to see from their facial expressions. Yet, that was the least of my concerns. I was glad that I had the chance to mentor students; that was all that mattered to me at that moment.

A few days later, a student I had met at the event e-mailed me. She thanked me for the invaluable advice that she had received that day and wanted to keep in touch. I am now her mentor and give her advice whenever needed.

It's good to share your experiences with others. Whenever I get the chance to be a role model, I try to go for events like this and give some advice on how to become a leader or how to be a better leader. Granted, I don't always get the time to do this, but I try my best to take out some time to mentor others.

Not long ago, I got to represent my Women in Leadership class online for my CIBE program. The university chose me and the brief article that I wrote about the subject to inspire others who were applying to the program. I was shocked that they would choose me!

When I spoke to one of the program managers, she told me, "You are amazing! You don't even realize it, but you have so much confidence and are a fine young woman. We were proud to choose you as you are the perfect example for our students."

"I guess I didn't realize my own potential!" I told her.

The program manager made me realize how others saw me as this amazing young businesswoman. It was a confidence-booster, but I always remind myself that it's ultimately what

I think of myself that matters and not what others do.

The way I got into the program was very unexpected. It was in June a few years ago that I came across a class that I liked. Without telling anyone, I applied for the class. Soon, someone from the program contacted me. "I think you would be a perfect fit for the CIBE program. What do you think?"

Excited at the amazing opportunity that had come to me, I applied for it. A few days later, the program manager for the Women in Leadership class contacted me. "We would love to have you in this class! Please do apply. I look forward to interviewing you soon."

Two phone interviews later, I got into the program. When I finally met these two program managers in person, they guided my mother and me in the right direction—towards completing this prestigious program. At twenty-nine, I graduated from the CIBE program and became an Ivy League graduate, something I never believed possible all those years ago. I was simply confident about myself and who I was. That's the secret to how I got in. Now, I'm a part of the Women's Circle alumnae group at the school.

The simplest way to help others is by donating old articles of clothing. Whenever I clear out my closet annually, I put aside whatever is old but still in wearable condition. I start by combing through my closet. "Will I still wear this?" I ask myself. "Will this look good on me?" If the answer to either of these questions is no, I simply put those clothes aside.

I then take all those clothes with me and give them to the

people I know who need them—either someone working for my family or a local charity that I know of. Although this is a small thing to do, it does help many others who may not be able to afford new clothes.

I go through my books, shoes, and costume jewelry as well. "Am I going to read this book again? Will anyone in the house read it?" I ask myself. If the answer is "no," I give those books to someone I know who likes to read but cannot afford to buy books. I even give my worn-out shoes to a person I know, and he or she happily uses them. When it comes to costume jewelry, I get rid of whatever has lost its luster and shine. I give it to someone I know, and they are happy to use that jewelry.

When it comes to buying new clothes, I make sure to buy things that will last a few years. I don't really do fast fashion as the quality is not always good, and you end up throwing that item after a few washes or uses. It also ends up being a waste of money.

If you buy one moderately expensive shirt as opposed to five high-street shirts, that one shirt will last for at least two years. You also save money when you only buy one shirt for eighty-five dollars as opposed to buying five shirts for a hundred dollars. It even helps the environment as you're buying less clothing that is eventually going to end up in a landfill.

I'm also quite picky when it comes to buying items for myself. There are times when I won't buy good quality but expensive items because I can find similar good quality items at the shops I know for a lower price. Now that's a bargain I like!

Buying excessive material things also means that you are using your money for things that may not necessarily be useful for you. Even if something is made by your favorite brand, this doesn't mean that you should buy it! It's better to keep your closet simple and your room clean.

The day my room is overloaded with too many things, I feel like my mind is also uneasy. I can never seem to find what I need, and things seem to magically disappear or get lost. It's better keeping things simple so that you can focus on other things, like your work.

When I initially started working from my home office, that room was filled with a lot of books, and some junk was lying around. I felt like I couldn't focus whenever I saw those books or other items. It was very chaotic and disorganized. Once I set up my home office in the new house that my parents moved to, I made sure that I had less clutter and more space.

Nowadays, I focus solely on my work. The bliss that I experienced by decluttering my office space has made a huge difference in the quality of my work. I now work even better than I did before and don't even realize how time goes by. That's how a workspace should be: neat, clean, and organized with just the essentials.

Helping others starts with you. When you know you're in a position to give advice or help others, take the chance to do so. It'll not only help you grow as a person but will impact others immensely. When you help others, you empower them as well. Do so with the goodness of your heart, and you will learn how to be grateful for what you have. That's how I learned to appreciate all that I have.

9

Accepting Things as They Are

Sometimes, things just refuse to work out the way we want them to, no matter what we do. At the same time, we may not have a choice; we have to face those incidents or uncomfortable situations head-on. When such an occasion arises, it's better to stay calm and accept that situation as it is. Soon enough, we learn to not only acknowledge the way things are going, but also adjust to those circumstances. We make the best of what we have right then.

When I was in college, I was paired with a roommate during one of my years at the student dormitory. She was nice enough to me in person and seemed to follow whatever guidelines we had initially set up. But things changed a month later, and I quickly learned that she didn't really like me. She came back to our dorm room quite late every day and studied into the early hours of the morning, with her bright desk lamp shining right into my eyes.

Once, she even came into the room with a friend of hers; both were highly intoxicated. When I woke up the next day,

I was surprised to see two people rather than one stirring in the bed next to me. As they giggled away, I realized it was my roommate and one of her friends—a girl about my age. I was a bit shocked that she had someone sleeping in the same bed, but I decided to go about my day as usual, without mentioning anything.

One day, my roommate started arguing with me. I don't remember how or why we started arguing, but before I knew it, she snapped and yelled at me, "You're so beautiful, rich, and smart. OF COURSE, I'M MAD!"

As a teenager, I was a bit alarmed at her outburst and didn't know what to say. I kept quiet and decided to go talk to the girl in charge of our dorm floor. "It's only a matter of a few months. I'm sure you can handle it till then because it's not going to be easy to find someone else to room with you now. It's almost the end of the school year. I hope you understand."

Needless to say, I had no choice but to stay with my roommate as there were just a few months left anyways. Things did get worse though. My roommate started to use my side of the room and my bed; she littered everywhere, and even left her dirty underwear on my bed. Once, I caught her going through my personal stuff and reading a book that I had recently bought. Although I didn't say much, other than the fact that she should not do this again, she knew I was quite upset with her childish behavior.

Fortunately, summer came, and I decided to move into a student apartment, which was a step up from the dorm that I was staying in. Occasionally, I did run into my roommate on campus, but we just smiled at each other and moved on. She gossiped and complained to our common friends about me while I said nothing about her. I figured that people knew the truth, so I didn't have to say anything. It was understood.

Because of her childish behavior, I learned to deal with any situation with confidence and diplomacy. Trust me, I was tempted to lose my cool and call her out on her behavior, but I knew she would have only made things worse (and she did, until the very end of our roommate days). She showed me how others saw me as a beautiful, rich, and smart girl who was everything that she was not. She wanted to be like me, and although she learned the hard way that we were poles apart, she used that as an excuse to vent her anger against me to our friends.

Whatever her excuse was for her behavior, I learned that putting someone else down doesn't make you look better; it just makes the other person look better while you look like an insecure coward.

My roommates at the student apartment were wonderful people whom I'm still in touch with today. The three of them were nice to me, and we all got along well. All of us were focused on our academic work in school, and two of them were going to graduate the year after.

Our year together was a brilliant experience. We all helped out when it came to cleaning the apartment.

"Hey, I did the dishes for you!" one of my roommates told me.

"Thanks, but you really didn't have to!" I told her.

Things like that happened frequently. Whenever they were busy, I would clean the apartment, and whenever I was busy, they would. It worked out well. We also gave each other enough space to study.

"The TV is too loud," I would tell them. "Could you lower the volume? I have an exam tomorrow."

"Sure thing!" one of my roommates said.

We were cordial and respectful towards one another. If someone had a problem, we would talk it out. We were all in sync with the things we did and with what we expected from each other. We had no expectations from one another as we knew that we were all focusing on our studies. We became good friends and would hang out together whenever we had free time. Although we were all vastly different in terms of our personalities and ethnicities, we got along well. We had one goal in common: to do our best in college.

If someone wanted to borrow something from the apartment, that was fine. If a guest was coming over, we would be informed of that. If the maintenance crew was coming to fix something, my roommates would let each other know. We were open about what had to be discussed, and we didn't have any problems with discussing any issues that we might have with each other.

That was one of my best years in college. It was also the year that I excelled academically and got into the Honors Program. When you have good, supportive people around you, things go well. Everything just flows in the right direction. Things start working out in your favor once you accept things as they are.

We all appreciated each other; we knew what bothered each other and what didn't. We expressed our feelings freely and did whatever we wanted to do, without anyone minding it. Our apartment was always clean, organized, and filled with laughter. Our friends loved stopping by, and we all had a wonderful time together. Of course, these roommates either graduated or moved out after one year, and a new set of roommates came in.

It was all okay with the new roommates until the day a very strange argument occurred. I was so busy with my schoolwork and academic clubs that I had forgotten to take out the garbage from the bathroom. I told my roommates that I would do it as soon as I got the chance to. But as it turned out, I forgot to take out the garbage that day and went for an exam the next day.

When I came home, I saw one of my roommates cleaning the bathroom. When she saw me, she dumped the trash can in front of my room; it was filled with dirty sanitary pads.

I saw all this take place in front of me and was a bit confused as to what had happened.

"Take out the trash, please," she told me.

"I was busy with my final exam. I totally forgot."

"Okay, but it's your job," she said. She then left the apartment.

I took out the trash.

A few days later, she messaged me, "Please clean the house today; it's dirty."

I knew we took turns cleaning the apartment, but I had already told her that I was a bit busy with my exams and would do so later.

That night, something unimaginable happened. As I was doing the dishes, my roommate started talking to me about something. Eventually, we had a full-blown argument; we were arguing about dishes and a number of other things.

All of a sudden, the topic of money came up. I have no idea how or why she wanted to talk about money, but she did. She said something that made me so upset that I secretly dialed my parents.

"YOU'RE CALLING YOUR PARENTS! UNBELIEVABLE!"

"No, I'm not..." I replied shakily. I ignored the call, and as she continued fighting with me, I lost my temper. "YOU KNOW I'M A FUCKING BILLIONAIRE!" I yelled at her.

Silence followed. What I had said was a massive exaggeration as we were just normal businesspeople with some money in hand, but her silly comments and behavior had really gotten to me. After a few tense minutes, we settled down.

"So, what does your family really do? Tell me," she laughed.

"Denim, manufacturing, chemicals..." I said. As I continued talking, her face grew sullen.

"Okay," she said.

My other roommate heard about this and sided with her. They were both racist and believed that people from developing countries had no money.

I decided to look for a new apartment without roommates, but it wasn't an easy task. The apartment lease didn't end until six months later, and I knew I couldn't stay with these two people anymore. They were making my life terrible and taking every chance they got to put me down because of my ethnicity.

Until that time, I had not really experienced the full extent of discrimination, but I did with these two roommates. They made me feel horrible for being a person of color—an American from a Third World country—and for having some money despite of this. For them, this made me revolting to the core.

I didn't conform to the stereotype that they had in mind. I didn't have an accent (private school does that to you), and my family was relatively known in the Indian business community. We had enough money to enable me to study abroad and spend on my basic amenities at school.

Just because these two roommates didn't want to believe the truth, their vindictive actions against me didn't make me less than what I was. I knew who I was and what I stood for, and I wasn't going to let their crazy antics affect my academic work at college.

Fortunately, I found an apartment that required no roommate, in a different building. I also found someone to replace me in the previous apartment, as required. When I started to pack all my belongings and furniture, my other roommate, who had remained silent during these arguments, came up to me.

"Leave these items here. They belong to us," she told me of the few kitchen rolls and toilet tissue rolls that I had bought recently for myself.

"Sure," I said.

I didn't care that I had bought those things, and I wasn't about to argue about toilet tissue early in the morning. I left the apartment with the movers and my bags and met my parents in the building lobby. No sooner had I gone out of the building and reached the café we were having lunch at than a text message arrived on my phone.

"She's leaving! YEAH!!!" One of my roommates had accidentally (or, at this point, purposely) messaged me and my other roommate.

My face dimmed, and my mother noticed.

"What happened?" she asked.

I showed her the message.

"Ignore it," she said.

The days went by, and I rarely saw my roommates around campus, even though one of them worked at the school café. I made sure that I stayed as far away from them as possible. But since we all were in the same school, I eventually ran into one of them at the café where she worked. I quickly went to a different counter and paid for my drink. She saw that I was using my own money and kept quiet.

The next day, when I went to my grandmother's house, I received an anonymous phone call in the middle of the night. I was working on one of my term papers, and noticed that my phone was ringing. Tired, I picked up the call.

"Shefali?"

"Yes," I said.

"GO HOME! GO HOME!!!! FUCK YOU!!!" The call ended.

Shaken, I checked my phone's caller ID. It said, "unknown caller." I ran to my grandmother's room and knocked on her door.

"Is everything okay?" she asked me, half asleep.

"My roommates just called me and threatened me," I told her.

"Okay, we'll figure this out tomorrow. Go to sleep. It's late."

The next day, I called the phone company, but to no avail. They said they could not identify who had called me as they had called from a blocked caller ID. I then took a hasty decision; I messaged one of the roommates online.

I said, "I know you guys called me yesterday night. You can't hide that. You threatened me. You guys are horrible people, and I hope you both learn a lesson from this."

She messaged me back denying the allegation, but I knew it was them. Who else would call and say such a thing?

A few months passed by. I wanted to put all of this behind me, so I sent her another message online.

"This is a month for forgiveness and for moving past things," I said. "I hope we can move past this and forgive each other."

She replied back, "Thank you. It's wonderful to hear that you have moved past all of this. All the best."

I never spoke to either of them again after that day.

From these two roommates, I learned an invaluable lesson indeed: knowing your self-worth and when to stand up for yourself. Had they not acted the way they did or said all of those belittling things to me, I would have kept quiet and dealt with it. Since I had no choice but to face this situation—as uncomfortable as it was—until I found a new apartment, I grew stronger as a person.

Nowadays, I really don't care if someone calls me too American, too Indian or whatever. I know who I am as a person, and I know my self-worth. What others say cannot and will not ever define me.

Life is a funny thing. Things just happen at times, and we have no choice but to accept them as they are. Once you learn to see the goodness in any situation, you learn to maintain a positive attitude in the best of times as well as the worst of times. You learn to balance out those little issues, and you also learn to appreciate the way certain things are done, even if someone does something you don't like.

Your anger simmers down, and you learn to become calmer. You're not so edgy anymore, and you get more opportunities in life. Things just start to work out, and you realize that life has its' ups and downs, but there's always a way through the worst of times. That's what makes us stronger and prepares us for whatever comes our way. We learn to be better leaders and make better decisions in times of stress. We grow as leaders and learn how to lead by accepting things as they are.

10

Go with the Flow

Sometimes you just have to go with the flow of things. That way, you keep changing and adjusting to the situation at hand. Frankly speaking, that means you sometimes have to accept the situation as it is. You also have to know who you are and your worth. You should own it! At the same time, you have to be humble and know when to show people who you really are.

During my wedding preparations, I had a few customized outfits made for myself through various designers. I had to meet the designers and decide what fabrics and colors to use as my input was needed for everything, down to the last-minute beading details. Some of my outfits took months to make, since they were embroidered by hand, and that meant that I had to go to the boutique for multiple fittings.

One of the final fittings took place during a busy day in the store. Much as we tried to make sure that no one else came in, it was impossible to do so, since it was the wedding season. I tried on my outfit at the back of the store, and the store assistant blocked the way to the changing rooms so that no one would see my outfit.

Soon, a line of people formed near that barrier, wanting to see which celebrity was trying their outfit on. Little did they know that it was just me. Since it was a customized bridal outfit, the designer and my parents said that no one was allowed to see it until I got married. That was certainly a day to remember; I will never forget the amount of random attention I got. I simply remained calm and let the store assistant handle the other people who were trying to see who it was.

"It's just a VIP," the store assistant told a customer who was trying to pry her way through the barriers. If it had been any other day, I probably would have been freaking out, but I knew I had to go with whatever was being told to me or else things could get out of hand.

A couple of months after my wedding, someone asked me if she could publish an article about my wedding. Her company, a well-known online publication, was interested in Indian weddings abroad. Since there were over a thousand guests at the wedding as well as musicians, singers, and beautiful outfits, the article is one of the most popular wedding articles on their site till date. People still talk about the wedding and its events even though its been over three years!

I was also invited to another special event—a glamorous fashion show by the designers who had customized my wedding reception outfit. It was one of the few shows that

I actually went to, since I normally don't go to such events, and it was a fabulous show. Filled with spectacular glitterati, it was the fashion event of the season in Mumbai. I wore a neon yellow and blue minidress.

As the valet opened my car and I got out, people looked at me. At first, I wasn't sure who they were looking at, but I realized soon enough that it was me. Granted, they saw me getting out of a fancy car with a chauffeur in front, but I never thought people would actually scrutinize and judge me the moment I walked into the spotlight. Luckily, I didn't get any pictures taken; I just went directly to the show in the hotel.

I walked through the golden doors to the show and sat in one of the front rows. The paparazzi were taking pictures of everyone, and one of the designer's assistants greeted me. The show was filled with breathtaking outfits, glamorous models, and some famous Bollywood personalities.

When I left the show, I met one of my friends there.

"You were at the show? I didn't see you," she said.

"I was at the front, near the main stage," I told her.

"Really? I don't believe you," she sneered.

"I was; the designers invited me," I told her bluntly.

"Sure," she said and walked away.

At first, I was surprised at my friend's remark, but then it hit me. She was jealous because I got to be at the front of the show while she had to sit all the way on the other side, far away from the paparazzi. Of course, the paparazzi weren't taking pictures of me, but who was I to tell her otherwise? I really didn't care that the designers had given me so much attention and that I had become a muse for them.

When my wedding got over, the designers actually posted two pictures from my wedding on their social media site, without mentioning my name, as per my request. I didn't want to get unwanted attention and fame from something I wasn't really interested in. I appreciated my fifteen minutes of fame, but I knew it was nothing more than that.

Although I got a lot of requests from my make-up artists, friends, designers, and other publications, I only did the bare minimum for them and asked that my full name not be mentioned wherever possible. Of course, I still get quite a bit of attention, since people keep asking me to post social media pieces for them from my wedding and from a few events that I recently attended.

Social events also tend to happen from time to time. I get invited to meet a few designers as well as to attend some special store events for VIPs only, but I try to avoid going for such things. I'm a quiet social butterfly who believes that silence should speak for itself.

At one event in the U.S., I got invited to meet a designer at a special store event. I waited patiently in line to meet her. All of a sudden, my personal shopper came up to me. "Come with me," she said, as she took my sister and me to the front. I got a limited-edition bag from the designer, and she signed it along with a blogger who had also designed the bag with her.

"Can I get a picture please?" a photographer asked.

"Sure," I said. I got a few pictures taken and then went off.

People were staring at me and whispering to each other, "Who's that girl? Is she famous? Do we know her?"

I was not famous. Neither did anyone really know me then. It was only because the store manager and personal shopper knew me that I got this unexpected VIP treatment from them. Such things do happen to me at times, but that's okay. I'd rather only take VIP treatment when it's offered. I would never ask to be treated better than anyone else, but I can't decline it when someone goes out of their way to do something nice for me.

Being a philanthropist, I also get invited to charity galas and events of that sort. I only attended one gala a few years ago while I was still doing my MBA, since they wanted to personally thank me for my contribution.

Glammed up in my finest designer dress, I attended the event. I sat at the table along with my mother who also attended the event. I spoke to the people around me and then left after a while. I had class the next day and couldn't stay for the whole event, but I was glad that I went.

I did get some attention from those sitting at the same gala table and from others whom I knew, but I knew that I did not need attention to be a philanthropist. Sure, it's nice to be told that you've done something good for the world, but it's really not necessary to show off who you are and what you can do for others, especially if they already know it.

"Let your work speak for yourself," my dad likes to remind me every once in a while. I do believe that you should be known for your work and not because you keep telling others about your work. Your work should speak volumes about your career. Silence speaks louder than words.

I accidentally became a muse because of my wedding celebration. A designer duo posted two social media posts about the event. I got to meet one of the designers before my wedding. He chose a color and theme for the outfit. He came back during my final outfit fitting in order to put the last few finishing touches for that.

"Can I please take a picture of you in this outfit?" he asked. "It'll be posted after the wedding."

"We'll get an actual picture at the wedding," said my mother.

A few days after my wedding, my mother sent the designer a picture of my sister, herself, and me in the designer's outfits. He instantly posted that on his social media page. Soon, the designer duo posted another picture from the wedding article that had been published about me. There I was, posted on their official social media page with almost a thousand likes in a few days, despite no mention of my full name, as per my request.

Soon, the online publication that had published my article

wanted to use another picture of me for the article they were writing about Indian weddings. And so, a second article came up. A year later, another article was published about Indians in the fashion industry, and my picture was posted along with my sister's (with our permission, of course), and that became the third article that had something about me in it. Although my full name was not mentioned (as per my request), people still took notice.

"Hey, can you please write a nice testimonial for me about the make-up I did for your wedding? Can I also have a few pictures?" asked my wedding make-up artist. She was a famous celebrity artist and wanted to showcase her work for my friends and her colleagues. A few days later, three posts went up on her main social media page, and three more posts were put up on her other social media page. Again, I requested her not to mention my full name, but still, people realized how many media posts were going up about me.

A year later, a friend of mine, who had designed my jewelry for one of the home wedding events, came over to our house.

"May I have a look at the wedding pictures?" she asked me.

"Sure," I told her.

As she saw the highlights from the video and photo albums, she paused to think for a moment. "Do you mind if I use your picture to showcase my jewelry?" she asked.

"I'd love that!" I told her.

A week later, she posted a picture from my wedding with just my first name on her main social media page, saying #model.

"I can't believe you used me as a model!" I told her. "Thank you."

Recently, my wedding planner posted a few pictures from my wedding on her social media page. Soon, she asked for my permission to tag me in a post that she wanted to share with me. I garnered quite a few likes for that, and it helped my wedding planner, who was also a friend of mine, to get some good publicity for her events company.

Granted, I had to put up a few posts for them as well as they asked me to do so, but I tend to just share posts with my family and friends. I don't like to show off or brag about anything. It's just not my thing. There's also so much work that I have to do at my real job that I really don't get such opportunities often.

Another make-up artist of mine met up with me a couple of months ago. While we were talking, she happened to mention that she needed some help with finding some more clients.

"How about we do a social media post?" I suggested.

"Yes, let's do that!" she said.

After a couple of tries, I finally got a social-media-worthy picture. After making sure the picture was good enough to post, I sent it to her. Sometime later, she posted it online.

"Thank you!" she told me.

The post got a few hundred likes. The next time I met her, we had already decided to post a few more pictures from the various events I was going for. I became a muse for her, and

I was glad that I was just being myself and helping someone out.

Being a muse comes with certain perks and responsibilities. I need to be a good role model for others as well as remain humble. I only take opportunities that are given to me and try to avoid asking for favors. Asking for favors is not something I like to do. If something does come up in the future, I wouldn't mind being a muse for a friend or someone else, if I'm able to help them out by doing so. Otherwise, it doesn't have any meaning for me.

Singing is something I'm very passionate about and good at too; it comes to me quite naturally. I participated in the school chorus from the time I was twelve and continued singing until the day I graduated with my Bachelor's degree.

I got to sing with a few other soloists during my high school graduation and continued honing my love for singing. When I was in college, I tried out for the chorus group on campus. I prepared myself to sing in front of a few others; I was excited to soon be a part of the group.

"Okay, you can sing now," the girl told me when I arrived for the audition.

I didn't know there were going to be quite a few people watching, and I grew a bit nervous. Still, I sang away.

The girl stopped me. "I don't really know this song. Let's try this song instead..."

Thrown off and even more nervous than before, I sang.

"We'll get back to you later," she said.

"I'm sorry but we can't accept you; you'll never be able to sing!" the girl wrote condescendingly in the e-mail she sent me the next day.

"Okay, so I failed. Now what?" I asked myself.

I noticed an opening in the University Choir and decided to audition for that. I got in as soon as I finished auditioning. I was chosen as a soprano I/II. The next day, I got on stage to sing with the other choir singers.

A girl came scurrying in right before we started to sing. As she stood next to me, I realized it was none other than the girl whom I had auditioned in front of for the campus choir group. She stared coldly at me and started singing. I joined in when my part came, and the look on her face was priceless. Her mouth hung open as she continued to look directly at me.

She left a few months later when she graduated, and a few years later, I got to sing as one of the soloists on graduation day. My audition as a soloist went well and my teacher was confident that I could sing with two other classmates.

Singing on stage that day, I had the time of my life. Everyone applauded. Had I listened to what that girl told me, I would have never sung on stage that day.

During my wedding reception in Dubai, one of the singers asked my husband and me to come on stage with him. My husband sang with the singer, and the singer turned to look

Own It!

at me, once my husband finished his lines.

"Repeat after me," he said.

This was unexpected, and I was unprepared for what was going to happen next. I was so nervous that I couldn't sing, and my sister sang for me instead.

"No, the bride has to sing," the singer said.

I built up my confidence and sang.

"Wow! You sing beautifully," the singer said.

As I continued to dance with the singers, I felt so happy.

When I climbed the stairs to go off stage, one of my guests said, "You have a wonderfully husky voice!"

"You can sing? I had no idea!" another guest told me.

"Melodious! You have a gorgeous voice," a friend of mine said.

Nowadays, I still practice singing with the help of my music teacher in Dubai. Maybe one day, I'll get the chance to sing at my sister's or friend's wedding. Who knows? Singing is my meditation.

Early on in my career, I learned to embrace myself, who I was and even who I was going to be. I also learned that fame can get to you if you're not careful. What I learned from my wedding was that you should go with the flow! If an opportunity came up, I seized it. I also learned that it's never too late to change. You can always try and be a better person than you were before, and when you are, more opportunities will come to you out of the blue.

"Please leave. GOODBYE!" one of my classmates wrote in my high school yearbook when I was in tenth grade. She was angry with me because I didn't really hang out with her in school, and I was immensely popular at my previous school. Not everyone was nice to me, and bullying made things worse. I struggled to find my identity as a global Indian American.

When I went to college, it was clear to me that I had to define who I was. No one else could define me. Once I came to terms with that, things became a little easier for me. The bullying decreased, along with my skin-picking. Since I turned thirty, my skin-picking is almost non-existent. Sure, it took a long time to become the confident leader that I am today, but good things don't come easy.

"Do you like being in the limelight?" a friend of mine recently asked me.

"I don't really care about that," I told him. "People know who I am, and I don't need to tell them. I'm just starting to make my mark on the world, and I know it's only the beginning for me. I know that more opportunities and responsibilities will come up."

Since I work in a public corporation, some amount of unexpected attention might arise. I only embrace opportunities that come my way, and I have learned to embrace the attention that comes with them. I learned the hard way that you can never force opportunities to happen. The process should be organic and natural; it shouldn't be something that you're chasing after. Otherwise, it definitely won't work.

A TV interview came up for me unexpectedly because a classmate of mine noticed my confidence and approached me. She asked me if I could be on her show. "You're so confident, you'd be perfect on the show!" she told me.

At first, I was a bit hesitant. What would I say? I told her this a few days later, and she actually started to guide me about what to do and say. With her help, I'm now preparing for my first interview.

Looking back at the way I was—an overweight kid with no confidence and no plans for the future—I can say with certainty that I have changed. It is because I kept adapting to everything that I became the leader that I am today.

Keep adapting, keep changing, and remember to embrace yourself! Own it. I keep climbing to new executive heights. One day, I'll make it to the top. I just know it. Keep believing in yourself, put aside the haters, and keep going. Don't look back and don't regret the mistakes you made. We're only human, after all. Remember that change is good, embrace your goals, know when to fight, and find the perfection in imperfection. Keep going, use anger as a tool, help others, accept things as they are, and go with the flow. The lessons you learn on this journey of change will stay with you forever.

Afterword

Thank you for reading my book. I hope it has inspired you just as I was inspired to write it. I wanted to share my story with the world so that I could empower others who are in a family business, through my life experience, the lessons I learned, and the challenges that I faced.

Now that you have learned the valuable lessons that I learned while becoming an executive at a young age, you should feel more confident about becoming a leader, no matter what your circumstances may be. I hope that you will not only learn to become a better leader but a better person as well.

I hope that I have made some difference in your life as this book has made in mine. That is my mission: to inspire and to be inspired. Keep inspiring and remember to own it!

About the Author

Shefali Karani (née Ramsinghani) is an Indian American who left the United States at the age of 5. She grew up in Mumbai, India and Dubai, U.A.E. With high expectations, she became an executive at the age of 21 at her family's corporate business in Mumbai. This was soon after she graduated with a Bachelor's degree, *cum laude* with distinction from Drexel University. During her Bachelor's program, she attended President Obama's inauguration with select students.

She also did the 1-Year MBA program at Drexel University. She got her CIBE from Columbia Business School in New York, and was a part of the Women in Leadership program. She's a part of the Women's Circle group at Columbia University.

Fulfilling the family business responsibilities, she's a board director for Rama Industries Limited (Gelatin), Rainbow Agri Industries Limited, and the BSE listed company Rainbow Denim Limited. She's an executive business director for the BSE listed companies Rama Phosphates Limited and Rama Petrochemicals Limited.

She resides in Dubai with her husband and travels for work. She continues to own it!

www.ingramcontent.com/pod-product-compliance
Lightning Source LLC
Chambersburg PA
CBHW032042290426
44110CB00012B/918